KV-354-078

Capt. H. McGuffie.
55 Loughborough Road.
Kirkcaldy
Fife.

THE COAL WAS THERE

FOR BURNING

The Coal was there for Burning

C. H. Milsom

MARINE
MEDIA
MANAGEMENT

Bibliography

For the history of the White Star Line and description of conditions in White Star ships of the late 19th century I have used the following:

A Book About Travelling, Past and Present, compiled· and edited by Thomas A. Croal (William P. Nimmo & Co., 1880).

Family Story, by Charles Drage (Stellar Press, 1970).

History of Merchant Shipping and Ancient Comme:ce, Vol. IV, by W. S. Lindsay (Sampson Low, Marston, Low & Searle, 1876).

The Atlantic Extra: Journal of the First Voyage of the Steamship Atlantic, edited by the Rev. A. A. Willits (White Star Line, 1871).

The Atlantic Ferry, by Arthur J. Maginnis (Whittaker & Co., 1892).

The Ismay Line, by Wilton J. Oldham (The Journal of Commerce, 1961).

Travelling Palaces, by R. A. Fletcher (Sir Isaac Pitman & Sons, 1913).

White Star, by Roy Anderson (T. Stephenson & Sons, 1964).

White Star Line Official Guide, 1877.

For details of the functions of the Board of Trade and for contemporary legislation:

Our Seamen, by Samuel Plimsoll (Virtue & Co., 1873).

Reports of the Royal Commission on Unseaworthy Ships (Blue Paper, preliminary 1873, final 1874).

Seafarers and Their Ships (H.M.S.O., 1966).

Ships of Peace, by P. G. Parkhurst (published by the author, 1962).

The British Mercantile Marine, by Edward Blackmore (Charles Griffin & Co., 1897).

The Ministry of Transport and Civil Aviation, by Sir Gilmour Jenkins (George Allen & Unwin Ltd., 1959).

And because I am not by profession either a nautical historian or a navigator I have leaned heavily on the following textbooks:

Dictionary of Marine Engineering and Nautical Terms, by G. O. Watson (George Newnes Ltd., 1964).

Dictionary of Nautical Words and Terms, by C. W. T. Layton (Brown, Son & Ferguson Ltd., 1955).

Nicholl's Seamanship and Nautical Knowledge, by Captain H. H. Brown (Brown, Son & Ferguson Ltd., 1966).

Seamanship for Junior Officers, by Captain R. M. Richardson (Brown, Son & Ferguson Ltd., 1963).

Bibliography

Additional technical details have been culled from *Memoir, Descriptive and Explanatory, of the Northern Atlantic Ocean and Comprising Instructions General and Particular for the Navigation of that Sea*, by Alexander George Findlay (Richard Holmes Laurie, 1873).

I have also consulted the annual report for 1873 of the Canadian Department of Marine and Fisheries, the *Nova Scotia Pilot*, the *Lights List*, 1873, and the following newpapers: *Illustrated London News, Liverpool Albion, Liverpool Daily Post, Liverpool Mercury*, the Halifax *Morning Chronicle, New York Tribune* and *The Times*.

On board the *Atlantic*, the new White Star boat,
  Five score of Yankees found themselves afloat . . .

The *Atlantic*! A name they'll ne'er forget,
  Though stranger scenes and climes may woo them—yet
In some warm corner memory still will keep
  A place for the *Atlantic* 'till life ends in sleep.

God bless her captain, officers and crew,
  Old England's sailors, ever bold and true,
And when we journey o'er the stormy brine
  We'll always travel by the White Star Line!

By a passenger on the *Atlantic's* maiden voyage, June, 1871

Dear friends, come listen to the tale,
  The loss which we deplore,
Of the gallant ship *Atlantic*, lost
  On Nova Scotia's shore.

O angry sea, give up thy dead,
  O rocky reef sink low.
How could you part so many friends?
  Why did you cause such woe?

O gallant ship that proudly sailed
  An hour before the shock,
Why did you not keep far away,
  And shun that sunken rock?

From a Nova Scotian ballad, April, 1873

Dedicated to the memory of Third Officer Cornelius Lawrence Brady, Able Seaman Edward Owen, Able Seaman John Speakman and Able Seaman Robert Thomas, whose courage and skill at the wreck of the *Atlantic* has never been adequately recognized.

©C. H. MILSOM, 1975

Published for The Institute of Marine Engineers
by
Marine Media Management Ltd.,
76 Mark Lane, London EC3R 7JN
(England Reg. No. 1100685)

Copyright © Marine Media Management Ltd.

This book is copyright under the Berne Convention. All rights reserved. Apart from any fair dealing for the purpose of private study, research, criticism, or review—as permitted under the Copyright Act 1956—no part of this publication may be reproduced, stored in a retrieval system or transmitted in any form or by any means, electronic, electrical, chemical, mechanical, optical photocopying, recording or otherwise without the prior permission of the copyright owners. All enquiries to Marine Media Management Ltd. at the above address.

ISBN: 0 900976 50 0

Printed in England by J. W. Arrowsmith Ltd., Bristol.

Introduction

THE loss of the British steamer *Atlantic* on the coast of Nova Scotia in 1873 was one of the worst marine disasters the world has ever known. Out of the 933 passengers and crew known to be on board (and there were possibly between 12 and 15 stowaways as well) 562 were lost. The 370-plus saved were all men; not one woman survived the wreck and the youngest child to be saved out of the many children and babies on board was a boy of 12. Like the other survivors, he owed his life to the courage and skill of the *Atlantic's* crew and the tenacity of the Nova Scotian fishermen who answered their call for aid.

Only the loss of the *Titanic* surpasses the horror of the wreck of the *Atlantic*, and it is perhaps not coincidence that both ships belonged to the White Star Line. The company led the way in trans-Atlantic travel for many years but their pioneering spirit took them along ways which others feared to sail until the course had been buoyed with the wrecks of foundered ships. "If blood be the price of admiralty, Lord God we ha' paid in full," might well be the epitaph of the White Star Line.

The *Atlantic* left Liverpool on a routine voyage, her 19th, to New York and many theories have been put forward to acount for her captain's decision to change course and proceed at full speed through the night to Halifax, Nova Scotia, a safe port when reached but a dangerous one to approach. That he was seeking shelter from the foul weather which had beset the ship all the previous week may be discounted. The *Atlantic* was a well-found ship and her officers had perfect confidence in her ability to weather a North Atlantic gale, but she lacked the modern aids of radar to see through the night to the rocks ahead, echo sounder to warn of the shallow water under her keel, and direction finder with which to fix her position, that are taken for granted today. But these are only aids to navigation and do not supplant the Mariner's Creed—Lead, Latitude, Lookout and Log. Had the crew aboard the *Atlantic* observed this creed they would have had no need for modern inventions, but no lead was cast to discern the depth, no latitude was ascertained with any accuracy, no lookout saw the breakers until it was too late, and the log on its own gave only a false sense of security.

For their negligence in the management of the ship the master and one of his officers were duly censured, and so, too, was the White Star Line. Whether that criticism of the company was justified is another matter and in the light of so many contradictory reports I have deemed it advisable to use as the basis of this work the depositions taken at the Halifax inquiry and the official report of that inquiry; the depositions taken at the Liverpool inquiry, the shorthand writer's report of that testimony, and the official reports which followed; and various letters which passed between the interested parties.

For details of the wreck, for illustrations and for many useful items of information I am grateful to:

Mr. Thomas E. Appleton, Historian, Marine Services, Department of Transport, Ottawa.

Miss Hilary A. C. Baker, R.A., Department of Pictures, National Maritime Museum.

Dr. E. Bruce Ferguson, Provincial Archivist of Nova Scotia.

Mr. R. J. Fisher, President of Pickford & Black Ltd., steamship agents of Halifax, Nova Scotia.

Mr. William H. Flayhart, III, of Lycoming College, Williamsport, Pennsylvania.

Mr. Alan Hedgley, Public Affairs Manager, Harland & Wolff Ltd., Belfast.

Mr. Neils W. Jannasch, Curator, Maritime Museum, Halifax, Nova Scotia.

The late Captain A. W. Kane, of Islandmagee, for drawing my attention to the part played by William Hoy, as described in *The History of Islandmagee* by Dixon Donaldson (published by the author, 1927) and to my friends Roy and Aileen Hawthorne for lending me a copy of this work.

Mr. M. R. Lownds, of the Canadian Broadcasting Corporation, Halifax, Nova Scotia.

Mr. D. J. W. McCarthy, of Marine Design Associates, of Palm Beach, Florida.

Mr. D. W. Morrison, of Edinburgh.

Captain E. O. Ormsby, R.C.N.R., district marine manager at Dartmouth, Nova Scotia, for the Canadian Ministry of Transport.

The staff of the Dominion Hydrographer, Department of Mines and Technical Surveys, Marine Science Branch, Ottawa, for helping to pinpoint the position of the wreck.

Although there is no doubt about where the *Atlantic* struck, a surprising number of names are used to describe the locality, even by those most intimately concerned. Marr's Rock, off Meagher's Island; a rock 50 yards from Meagher's Islands; Marr's Head; Marr's Island; and Meagher's Rock are some of the names most commonly used, except by the inhabitants of Prospect, Nova Scotia, who, in 1873, at least, insisted it was the Golden Rule Rock which the ship struck. Neither Admiralty nor Canadian charts show a Meagher's Island but Mars Head is situated on Mosher Island and the Canadian Permanent Committee on Geographical Names suggests, without certainty, that Mosher Island was owned by Mr. John Meagher. That the numerous offshore islands in the vicinity of Prospect may have been known by the name of their principal inhabitant is borne out by the fact that a number of survivors were cared for by a local magistrate, Mr. Edmund (or Edward) Ryan, J.P., and Ryan Island lies to the north of Mosher Island.

Confusion over the name may also have been caused by the way in which shorthand reporters transcribed the spoken word "Meagher." I am grateful to Mr. Walter Lord, of New York, and to his secretary, Florence Gallagher, and her friend, Beatrice Meagher, and also to Mrs. W. J. Meagher, of Birkenhead, for telling me, among other things, that the Irish surname Meagher is pronounced Marr. To add to the confusion, however, there is a Meagher's Beach near Halifax which is known locally as Major's Beach.

For details of awards, and lack of awards, I am indebted to the Board of Trade, the Central Chancery of the Orders of Knighthood, the Liverpool Shipwreck and Humane Society and the Royal Humane Society.

Because I am not an engineer I have been glad of assistance from Mr. Alastair White, head of the marine engineering department of the South Shields Marine and Technical College.

For many of the books and newspapers mentioned I am grateful to the staff of Birkenhead Central Library and Liverpool Central Library. In this connection, also, I am indebted to the late Mrs. Marjorie Mougne, formerly librarian of the Seafarers Education Service in Liverpool, and especially to Mr. Craig J. M. Carter, editor of *Sea Breezes*, for allowing me full use of his magazine's extensive files and nautical library.

Introduction

The introductory verses are taken from *The Atlantic Extra* and were written by Mr. Philip S. Justice, one of the passengers on the ship's maiden voyage. The verses from the Nova Scotian ballad *The Wreck of the Atlantic* are three out of the 49 remembered by Robert Langille, of Tatamagouche, Colchester County, Nova Scotia, and are reprinted by permission of the Harvard University Press from *Ballads and Sea Songs of Nova Scotia* by W. Roy Mackenzie. The verses by the Hon. Winifred E. Rollo are taken from *The History of Islandmagee*.

Each illustration bears an acknowledgement of its source, but I would like to thank particularly Mr. Peter Williams, of Amlwch, Anglesey, who went to so much trouble to copy a lithograph in his possession.

It hardly needs to be added that the persons mentioned here are not responsible in any way for the manner in which I have used the advice they offered, and if I have erred then the fault is mine alone. The words spoken by persons named in the text are the actual words which they themselves admitted afterwards to having used. The only licence to which I have resorted is in the reconstruction of the conversation between the master and the chief engineer which took place in the *Atlantic's* chartroom shortly before she made her fateful alteration of course to Halifax. Both officers repeated the substance of this conversation on oath, but each contradicted the other. I have chosen to believe that the master was so engrossed in the navigation of his ship that he failed to hear what the chief engineer said to him.

The reader may decide for himself whether or not this is a reasonable assumption.

C. H. MILSOM

Contents

Chapter One

A Reputation for Safety

"*Atlantic* mistook lights and struck rocks near Halifax, 2 a.m. Tuesday; rolled over into deep water; sank immediately; 250 saved themselves by clinging to rigging; were taken off by fishermen; 700, including women and children, drowned; no names known as yet; survivors will be landed at Halifax, Wednesday afternoon, cared for by Cunard."

I T was a difficult telegram for Thomas Henry Ismay to compose on that morning of April 2, 1873; a hard thing to admit to the Board of Trade that one of *his* ships had suffered the same fate as those of so many of his contemporaries. The public's memory was long, even without newspaper files to remind them, and it was not many years since the American liner *Arctic* had foundered in the North Atlantic with the loss of more than 300 lives. Some 60 members of the crew, and 23 male passengers, had survived on that occasion, but not one woman or child. The Collins Line had surmounted the loss of their fastest and finest liner, but the disappearance two years later of their *Pacific* put an end to the company. Now Ismay feared for his White Star Line.

It was a time of great agitation for an increased measure of safety at sea. In 1872, the year before the *Atlantic* was wrecked, 704 British ships were lost due to stranding, 242 foundered, 79 failed to arrive at their port of destination and were listed as missing, another 60 sank after collision and 63 were lost due to "other causes". The loss of these 1,148 ships, which excluded fishing vessels, cost the lives of 2,073 seamen and 105 passengers. In the first six months of 1873 the figure for passengers lost rose to 793, most of whom had been on board the *Atlantic*.

It was at this time that Samuel Plimsoll published *Our Seamen*, in which he sought to show, by words, charts and pictures, that "a great number of ships are sent to sea in such rotten and otherwise ill-provided state that they can only reach their destination through fine weather . . .".

Plimsoll, a successful manager of a brewery in Yorkshire and an unsuccessful coal merchant in London, was a born agitator. When he took up arms against the "mercenary and murderous greed" of the shipowners he possessed all the ingredients necessary for a vigorous campaign—a popular cause, pungent wit, ready tongue, and an ability to bend the facts when it seemed that a little bending would strengthen his case. He had little regard for accuracy and saw nobody's point of view but his own, but a generous and sympathetic public were prepared to believe his case that shipowners preferred their ships to sink so that they could collect the insurance money, rather than stay afloat and return a steady profit from passengers and cargo.

Plimsoll entered Parliament in 1868 and in 1871 he introduced his Merchant Shipping (Survey) Bill, calling for the adoption of a maximum loadline and the compulsory survey of certain classes of ship. Experts in the Marine Department of the Board of Trade said the Bill was "too silly to require minute examination" and it was withdrawn, but not before the Marine Department had noted its salient points. Later in the year they introduced their own Merchant Shipping Bill which, when it became law, made it an offence to send unseaworthy ships to sea.

Plimsoll was far from satisfied, and largely as a result of his agitation the Government appointed a Royal Commission on Unseaworthy Ships under the chairmanship of the Duke of Somerset. The Order setting out the commission's terms of reference was dated March 29, 1873—four days before the *Atlantic* ran at full speed on to the coast of Nova Scotia. No time is opportune for a shipwreck, but Ismay might be forgiven for thinking that some times are less opportune than others, and certainly April, 1873, was not a time when a shipowner wanted one of his ships bathed in the limelight of disaster.

For Ismay it was a particularly hard blow. Not only did he pride himself on the safety and comfort of his White Star liners, but had found that safety was a good selling point in a highly competitive industry. Under the title *Regulations for the Safe and Efficient Navigation of the Company's Steamships*, he wrote, in January, 1872: "The commanders must distinctly understand that the issue of the following instructions does not, in any way, relieve them from the entire responsibility for the safe and efficient navigation of their respective vessels; and they are also enjoined to remember that, whilst they are expected to use every diligence to secure a speedy voyage, *they must run no risk which might by any possibility result in accident to their ships. It is to be hoped that they will ever bear in mind that the safety of the lives and property entrusted to their care is the ruling principle that should govern them in the navigation of their ships, and no supposed gain in expedition, or saving of time on the voyage, is to be purchased at the risk of accident.**

"The company desires to establish and maintain for its vessels a reputation for safety, and only looks for such speed on the various voyages as is consistent with safe and prudent navigation."

These regulations were not only framed for the benefit of the company's masters and officers; copies were made freely available to the travelling public so that all might know that in White Star ships, the comfort and safety of the passengers was of paramount importance. But there were other considerations as well, and 12 months after issuing the regulations, Ismay sent a circular order to all the masters in his fleet.

"In the book of instructions handed to you some time ago," he wrote, "and with the contents of which we do not doubt you have made yourself familiar, we dwelt with particular emphasis upon the supreme importance which we attached to the exercise of extreme and unvarying prudence in the navigation of the company's vessels; but so much has this subject weighed upon our minds of late, that we have determined to address you again in regard of this most vital subject.

"The consideration of the subject generally has impressed us with a deep sense of the injury which the interests of the company would sustain in the event of any misfortune attending the navigation of their vessels; first, from the blow which such would give to the reputation of the line; second, to the pecuniary loss which would accrue, the company being their own insurers to a considerable extent; and third, to the interruption of a weekly line, upon which much of the success of the present organization must depend.

* (Ismay's italics)

A Reputation for Safety

"Under all these circumstances of paramount and engrossing interest to the company, whose property is under your charge, we write to you to dismiss from your mind all idea of competitive passages with other vessels, the advantage of success in which is merely transient, concentrating your whole attention upon a cautious, prudent and ever watchful system of navigation, which shall lose time or suffer any other temporary inconvenience rather than run the slightest risk which can be avoided."

With the loss of the *Atlantic* less than two months after this order was circulated, Ismay saw his fears realized, but even worse was to follow. The *Atlantic* had been bound for New York, but she ran aground near Halifax, 600 miles to the north east. Ismay might possibly have forgiven an error in navigation, although his rules clearly stated: "A wide berth to be given to all headlands, islands, shoals, and the coast generally . . . " but he could not overlook the allegation that "parsimony and culpable negligence in the management at Liverpool" allowed the *Atlantic* to sail so short of coal that she had to put into the nearest port to restock her bunkers.

"Such culpable dereliction of duty approximates more to murder than to manslaughter," stated the father-in-law of one of the dead passengers. "So sweeping a sacrifice of upwards of 600 lives from causes so entirely within the control of those owning and navigating the ship ought, for the credit of the Government of this great country, to be thoroughly investigated."

Ismay welcomed an investigation as the one thing which, while perhaps emphasizing the carelessness of the officers in his employment, would help, he thought, to uphold his company's reputation for operating well-found, well-equipped ships. There was yet a chance that something might be saved on which to build the future of the White Star Line.

Chapter Two

Thomas Henry Ismay

ISMAY was a descendant of John de Ayketon and Isemaye, his wife, who owned land in her own right near Carlisle in the 13th century. The family remained landowners and farmers in Cumberland until the Thomas Ismay, born at Uldale in January, 1755, decided to seek his fortune at sea. Captured by the French during the Napoleonic Wars, he died at Guadeloupe but his son, Henry, rose to command a small ship built and owned by Joseph Middleton, of Maryport.

Henry Ismay married Middleton's daughter, Charlotte, left the sea and established a grocery business in Maryport. Henry and Charlotte's second child, Joseph, became a foreman shipwright in his uncle Isaac Middleton's shipyard and married a local girl, Mary Sealby. Joseph and Mary Ismay lived in a small cottage in Whillan's Yard, a passage between Wood Street and John Street, and there, on January 7, 1837, Thomas Henry Ismay was born.

When Thomas was 10 years old his father left the shipyard and established himself as a timber merchant, shipbuilder, shipbroker and, with a share in a number of ships trading into Maryport, a shipowner. Joseph Ismay prospered and his son was sent to Croft House School, near Carlisle, one of the best boarding schools in the North of England.

Joseph died while the young Ismay was still at school and it was his great uncle, Isaac Middleton, who took the next step by apprenticing him to Imrie, Tomlinson & Co., a firm of shipbrokers in Liverpool.

Before he was 21, Ismay left Imrie, Tomlinson & Co. to go into partnership with a retired shipmaster, Captain Philip Nelson, who also came from Maryport and who owned one ship, the *Ann Nelson*. Nelson & Co. became Nelson, Ismay & Co., shipbrokers, with offices at No. 21, Water Street, Liverpool. The partnership prospered, and two years later they commissioned Alexander Stephen & Sons to build an iron brigantine for them. This ship, the *Angelita*, was followed quickly by the *Mexico*, the *Ismay* and the *Arriero*, but in January, 1862, Ismay suffered a foretaste of what was to come. The *Angelita* was wrecked off the coast of Ireland, Nelson retired, and Ismay was left to carry on alone, trading now as T. H. Ismay & Co., from offices at No. 10, Water Street.

Up to this time, Ismay had concentrated on the West Indian and Mexican trade, but within a year of becoming his own master he joined the board of the National Steam Navigation Co., which traded into New York.

Also running out of Liverpool at this time were the sailing ships of Pilkington & Wilson, founded in 1845 and now trading successfully to Australia as the White Star Line. In 1854, Pilkington & Wilson suffered a severe setback with the loss of the ship *Tayleur* which they were handling for Charles Moore & Co., but undaunted they took on charter the clipper *Red Jacket*, a vessel noted for her speed and only outraced by the *Cutty Sark* herself.

4

Pilkington & Wilson saw a good omen in the *Red Jacket* for her figurehead was a Red Indian chief and on his breast was painted a white, five-pointed star. But the race was on, clipper against clipper, clipper against steam, and by 1856 Pilkington had had enough of the cut-throat competition of the shipping business. He retired, and Wilson went into partnership with his brother-in-law, James Chambers, and the firm became H. T. Wilson & Chambers.

And so now the White Star Line entered the steam trade, but like Pilkington before him, Chambers had no stomach for international shipping, and was replaced in 1865 by John Cunningham. Early the following year, Pilkington and Chambers had reason to be glad they had quit the business. Barned's Bank failed and the mortgages they held for most of the White Star Line's ships were taken over by the Royal Bank of Liverpool. Wilson & Cunningham owed the bank over £500,000 and when, in 1867, the Royal Bank also crashed, the partnership was dissolved. Seizing the chance, Thomas Ismay stepped in and for £1,000 bought the White Star insignia and the company's goodwill in the Australian and New Zealand trade. Perhaps with it he captured Pilkington & Wilson's original dictum, that their primary objective would be "to study the safety as well as the comfort of the passengers under their charge".

Two years later Ismay formed an association with the Belfast shipbuilding firm of Harland & Wolff, a move which was to establish the White Star Line firmly on the prestige North Atlantic route.

E. J. Harland, later Sir Edward Harland, Bart., was born at Scarborough in May, 1831, the sixth child of a family of eight. At the age of 15 he was apprenticed to Robert Stephenson & Co. at Newcastle-upon-Tyne and when he finished his time he started work with J. & G. Thompson, engine builders, of Glasgow. Later he returned to the Tyne, but was dissatisfied with the prospects offered by his employers and in 1854 applied, successfully, for the post of manager with Robert Hickson & Co., iron shipbuilders, of Belfast. Three years later, Hickson learned that his energetic manager intended setting up on his own account, and offered him the Belfast shipyard for £5,000.

The transfer was completed with the assistance of a Liverpool merchant, Gustavus C. Schwabe, who was an old friend of Harland and the uncle of his private assistant, Gustav William Wolff. Wolff was an able engineer and had had considerable experience at sea, and as the new firm's business expanded, Harland offered him a partnership. This took effect in April, 1861, with Harland putting up £1,916 of the firm's capital and Wolff £500.

Harland was a clever and daring designer. He built ships longer than they had ever been before without increasing the beam, so as to obtain greater carrying capacity. He made the upper deck entirely of iron, so that the hull was converted into a box girder of immensely increased strength. He made the keel flat and the bilge square, a design which was known in Liverpool as the Belfast bottom. These ships were built for J. Bibby, Sons & Co., and were also called Bibby's coffins, because of their shape, but in service they proved themselves fast, economic and possessed of good stability.

Gustavus Schwabe also knew Thomas Ismay, and in 1869 he suggested that if Ismay formed a company to operate a trans-Atlantic service with iron ships, he, Schwabe, would back the company as long at its ships were built by Harland & Wolff. Ismay agreed, and in conjunction with G. Hamilton Fletcher, a shipowner in his own right and a fellow director of the National Steam Navigation Co., the Oceanic Steam Navigation Co. was formed on September 6, 1869, with Ismay contributing a large part of the £400,000 capital.

He was then 32 years old, 10 years married and the father of three small children. And, as agreed, the first act of the new company was to place an order with Harland & Wolff for four steamers to be built of iron to a design by Harland. The first was to be called *Oceanic*, the second *Atlantic*, the third *Baltic* and the fourth *Pacific*, but before the last-named was launched (without ceremony, like all White Star ships) Ismay was reminded that a Collins liner with this name had been lost without trace, and the name *Republic* was substituted for *Pacific*.

All four ships were to be of similar design, the later ones to be modified as necessary, according to the experience gained with the first. They were to be vessels of 3,700 gross tons, 2,366 register, 420 ft long and 40 ft beam. The compound inverted engines, made by G. Forrester & Co., of Liverpool, were to drive a single screw and were designed to develop 600 horsepower (3,000 i.h.p.). These engines had two high-pressure cylinders each 41 in in diameter, and two low-pressure, each 78 in in diameter, working on two cranks with a stroke of 5 ft.

Each high-pressure and low-pressure cylinder formed a complete engine in itself and could be used as such in the event of a breakdown of the other pair. Steam at a designed pressure of 70 lb was generated in 10 boilers each having two furnaces, and there was a donkey boiler for driving the deck machinery which could also be connected with the main boilers.

The bunkers were designed to hold 798 tons of coal stowing at 45 cub ft to the ton and it was estimated that 40 tons of coal per day would drive the ship at $10\frac{1}{4}$ knots, 56 tons would achieve 14 knots and 60 tons would produce a maximum speed of $14\frac{1}{2}$ knots. In addition to the engines there were to be masts and sails—fore, main, mizzen and jigger, square rigged. There was to be a steering engine worked by steam and operated from a wheel amidships, and a secondary steering wheel aft operated by a barrel purchase. There were to be three bower anchors of Trotman design, the largest weighing 55 cwt, a stream anchor of 57 cwt, three Trotman kedge anchors and four boat anchors. Chain cables, hawsers and warps, leads and lines, were to be of the best quality.

For safety reasons there were to be 12 lifebuoys and 76 lifebelts—not enough for all on board but more than required by law. Two guns of 6 in bore were to be fitted for the firing of distress signals and there was to be a fog horn and a bell. Ten lifeboats were to be fitted capable of carrying 600 people—more, again, than the law required—and they were to be equipped with Murray's lowering apparatus so that they could be put into the water in four and a half minutes.

There were to be pumps for moving water out of the ship and 420 ft of fire hose for pouring water into the ship.

There was to be accommodation for 166 first-class passengers in the saloon and 952 emigrants in the steerage, and a crew of 142.

Edward Harland once said that quality was "a very important element in all commercial success", and it was quality that Ismay was striving after. Harland & Wolff were given *carte blanche* to build the best possible ships, irrespective of expense, Ismay agreeing to pay the cost price plus a percentage which would represent the builders' profit; for the *Atlantic* the overall cost totalled £120,000.

It was a system which worked well, and which produced remarkable ships, and so close became the ties between builder and owner that Ismay agreed not to obtain ships from any other yard while, in return, Harland & Wolff agreed not to build ships for any company in competition with White Star. It was a relationship which even survived the interference of the owner in the plans of the designer, for Ismay knew what he wanted and he was determined to get it. And in the long run, it was his ideas which made the *Oceanic* class so successful that they rendered obsolete every other ship on the North Atlantic.

Previously, passenger accommodation had been contained within the hull, with one or more houses built onto the upper deck. Because these deckhouses were subjected to the full brunt of the weather, their portholes were small and they were often both dim and dank. Harland & Wolff, at Ismay's instigation, joined the roofs of the deckhouses together and extended them out level with the side of the ship, supporting them with stanchions.

The effect was to provide a promenade deck on top of the deckhouses which in turn, by being joined together, became spacious accommodation for the passengers. A ship today may have a tier of decks but it was a revolutionary breakthrough in naval architecture when someone did it for the first time.

The *Oceanic* class were also remarkable for being the first ships built without bulwarks. These were considered necessary to keep water off the decks, but with a high sea running not even the highest bulwark could keep the deck dry, and the bulwarks were fitted with scuppers through which the water could drain away over the side. In practice, the scuppers could seldom cope quickly enough with a heavy sea and the bulwarks served to retain the water, swilling about on deck. Instead of bulwarks, therefore, the *Atlantic* had railings of sufficient height to prevent the passengers falling over the side, but open to allow water to drain away as quickly as it poured in.

Ismay had noted, too, that one of the elements contributing towards seasickness (the bane of trans-Atlantic travel before the days of preventive medicine and stabilisers) was vibration from the engines, and he had found that vibration was most noticeable abaft the engine-room, along the line of the propeller shaft. He therefore moved the first-class accommodation away from its traditional place aft and placed it amidships. The saloon extended from one side of the ship to the other and was lit by large, airy skylights and larger portholes than had ever been fitted in a ship before. An ornate stairway connected the saloon with the promenade deck above.

The first-class passengers' rooms were on the same deck as the saloon and extended aft along either side of the engine-room casing and forward on either side of the cargo hatches. Every room had a large porthole and for the first time, each room was connected to an electric bell system "and a touch of the finger to the ivory disc", said a passenger, "commands the instant notice of the attendants".

While the *Atlantic* was being built she was inspected periodically by surveyors from the Underwriters' Registry of Iron Vessels, a society conducted by a joint committee of underwriters, shipowners and shipbuilders and represented in Liverpool by their chief surveyor, James Wimshurst. When she was completed, in November, 1870, Wimshurst issued a certificate which stated: "This vessel was built under the special inspection of the Surveyors for the Underwriters' Registry of Iron Vessels, and in her hull, decks, rigging, spars, sails, anchors and chains, is a First Class vessel, fit to carry dry and perishable cargo, and classed for a period of 20 years from the date of launching, subject to survey every four years if the vessel be in the United Kingdom."

At this time, the White Star Line was managed by T. H. Ismay & Co., & Fletcher, but when William Imrie, of Imrie, Tomlinson & Co., died his son, William, decided to pool his resources with his old friend Thomas Ismay. The new firm of Ismay, Imrie & Co. became managers of the Oceanic Steam Navigation Co., operating steamers on the North Atlantic under the direction of Ismay and Fletcher, and of the North Western Shipping Co., operating sailing ships under the direction of Imrie.

Chapter Three

Preparation for Final Voyage

T HE *Atlantic* made her first voyage in the summer of 1871 and for as little as 16 guineas one way or 27 guineas return, first-class passengers were offered amenities never before associated with passenger ships. Overnight, she became the most popular ship on the North Atlantic run, and so impressed were the saloon passengers on that maiden voyage that they prevailed upon one of their number, the Rev. A. A. Willits, of Philadelphia, to write a comprehensive account of the voyage.

"The splendid accommodation of the ship," he wrote, "the charming weather, the distinguished and talented character of the company on board, and the novel, instructive and delightful entertainments in the saloon every evening during the passage have together made this a most remarkable and memorable voyage; so much so, that many gentlemen on board, who have crossed the ocean repeatedly, declared they had never seen anything comparable with it before, and that it really initiates a new era in ocean navigation."

Most of the passengers were American, and Independence Day was celebrated in a manner which met with their whole-hearted approval, marred only by an accident to the arms of one of the quartermasters when firing a salute from the *Atlantic's* signal gun. But one of the passengers, Dr. J. Marion Sims, amputated both his hands and the rest of the passengers collected £150 for him, so even that did not spoil the Rev. Willits' eulogy. The White Star Line liked it so much that they published it in the form of a brochure, but after the *Atlantic* had been wrecked all copies were withdrawn and in the company's subsequent literature the name of the ship was not even mentioned; it is as though she had never existed.

One passenger, Mr. Hepworth Dixon, likened "these passage boats" to "a floating palace, with the style and comfort of a Swiss hotel".

"After trying her for several days and nights," he said, "in weather of the roughest sort, even at the equinoxes, I am ready to despair of finding any vessel more completely to my mind. A floating palace with 500 souls, we measure more than 400 ft in length, and have a saloon amidships, gay with gold and soft with cushions, in which the young ladies can flirt and their elders dawdle over books and prints. The smoothness is remarkable, and the ventilation perfect, with the exception of one evening when we held a concert; we breathe a fresh and bracing air that gives a wonderful keenness to the palate.

"We have a host of little comforts, some of which are not to be had in a first-class Swiss hotel. We have a good piano, and a real library of books, a smoking-room, a barber's shop, and a ladies' room. Each passenger has a printed list of his fellows, and a track chart of the ferry, so that he knows the persons on his right and left, and keeps a daily check on the officer who marks our log. The crew is perfect, from the captain, in whose skill and vigilance we put our deepest trust, down to his boy, Tommy, a young and laughing scapegrace, who attends my own particular berth, and sees that there is plenty of iced water in my jug."

Dixon also drew attention to the fact that ships of the White Star Line followed the routes recommended by Lieutenant Matthew Fontaine Maury, of the United States Navy. "These lanes," said Ismay, "if generally adopted, would, I think, materially lessen the risks of collision and of ice." It was another example of his striving for perfect safety for his ships and those who sailed in them, and the masters of White Star liners were instructed to follow Maury's routes "as being generally acknowledged to constitute the safest and most reliable courses for all seasons of the year".

So concerned was Ismay with maritime safety that he did not hesitate to tell his fellow shipowners when he considered their vessels were being navigated without due caution. The *Atlantic* sailed from Liverpool on her sixth voyage in November 1871, with orders to proceed as far as Queenstown at reduced speed, and to carry no sail. The Inman liner *City of Paris* sailed half an hour later and, with sails set to aid her engines, gradually overhauled the *Atlantic* on her starboard side. The *Atlantic* had the Skerries close on her port side, giving her very little room in which to manoeuvre, but all would have been well had the *City of Paris* maintained her course. Instead, as she drew ahead, she cut across the bows of the *Atlantic* at a distance estimated by the *Atlantic's* master to be 50 to 60 yards. Had anything carried away aboard the *City of Paris* as she crossed over she would almost certainly have been run down by the *Atlantic*.

The Regulations for Preventing Collisions at Sea, forerunner of the present International Collision Regulations, then formed Part IV of the Merchant Shipping Act, 1854, and had been in force since June 1, 1863. Article 17 of these regulations stated that every vessel overtaking any other vessel should keep out of the way of the vessel being overtaken; in other words, the *City of Paris* should have kept out of the way of the *Atlantic*.

From his master's report of the incident, Ismay considered that the *City of Paris* had acted in a way fraught with considerable danger, and he wrote to William Inman, owner of the ship, to tell him so.

"We feel convinced," he said, "that you cannot be aware of this very unwise and hazardous course on the part of the officer in charge of your boat; and we are likewise sure that you will take prompt and decisive measures to prevent the recurrence of such a proceeding on a future occasion; at the same time, we consider it but just to ourselves to state that we have enjoined the masters and officers under our charge to act on all occasions even in excess of mere prudence to avoid the possibility of danger, regardless of any loss of time thereby involved, which, in comparison with the safety of life and property, we deem to be wholly unimportant."

Before sailing on her 11th voyage, in May, 1872, the *Atlantic* had a new propeller fitted, but the chief engineer reported that it caused excessive vibration throughout the ship. "At the after stuffing box (the space surrounding the propeller shaft, filled with packing to make a pressure-tight joint) it is fearful," he said, "and the engines when making 35 revolutions per minute, appear to oscillate about an inch at the starting platform."

By the end of the year the White Star Line ships had suffered nine broken propeller blades within a space of two months, and on December 20, Ismay brought the problem to the attention of Harland & Wolff. "Constant breakage of the propeller blades," he wrote, "is becoming a question of the most serious importance to us, not only on account of the great expense entailed thereby, but also affecting the prestige of the line, which must suffer if these accidents continue."

Ismay had also been at great pains to obtain a design of ship in which the passengers would not suffer the discomfort of excessive vibration from the engines, and before setting out on her 17th voyage, in January, 1873, the *Atlantic* entered one of the Mersey Docks and Harbour Board's public drydocks in the Great Float, Birkenhead, to have her three-bladed propeller changed for one with four blades, in the hope that this would prevent the vibration and also reduce the risk of breakage.

While in drydock she was inspected by William Quiggin and Daniel Mylchreest, shipwright surveyors then employed by the Board of Emigration Commissioners. Prior to 1851 the only surveyors of ships were those employed by the classification societies such as Lloyd's Register of Shipping, but in that year the Steam Navigation Act gave the Board of Trade the power to appoint surveyors of their own, instead of merely approving their appointment.

Quiggin and Mylchreest held their positions with the Board of Emigration Commissioners under an Act of 1852 which had been laid down in an attempt to alleviate the terrible conditions under which emigrants were often carried. The Board of Emigration Commisioners were appointed under the direction of the Secretary of State for the Colonies but in January, 1873, the powers both of the Commissioners and of the Secretary of State with regard to passenger ships were transferred to the Marine Department of the Board of Trade. The transfer made no difference to Quiggin's or Mylchreest's duties; they simply became responsible to another Government department.

It was the surveyor's duty to see that passenger ships, at least, complied with certain prescribed standards. Under the consolidating Merchant Shipping Act of 1854 they were empowered to go aboard every vessel classed as a passenger ship at intervals of six months "to inspect the same, or any part thereof, or any of the machinery, boats, equipments or articles on board thereof". Having carried out their inspection, the surveyors furnished the owners of the ship with a report, and the owners, in return, sent the report to the Board of Trade.

If the Board were agreed that the report was a satisfactory one and that the ship complied with the Act, a certificate was issued to the owners which had to be displayed in some conspicuous part of the ship so as to be visible to all persons on board.

If the ship put to sea without a valid certificate, the owner was liable to a fine not exceeding £100 and the master to a fine not exceeding £20. Not until the Unseaworthy Ships Act of 1875 and the Merchant Shipping Act of 1876, following further agitation by Samuel Plimsoll, were the surveyors given real power to detain a ship if "by reason of the defective condition of her hull, equipments, or machinery, or by reason of overloading, or improper loading she is unfit to proceed to sea without serious danger to human life . . .".

Quiggin and Mylchreest, in 1872, did not have the benefit of this legislation, but as far as the *Atlantic* was concerned, they did not need it. Quiggin, particularly, knew ships; he had been a builder of iron and wooden vessels himself for 30 years before joining the Board of Emigration Commissioners and he had never seen one as staunch as the *Atlantic* and her sisters.

His last survey of her, made on December 23, 1872, in drydock and on January 7, 1873, afloat, was not a particularly searching one because it was the White Star Line's practice to drydock their ships regularly in order to scrape their bottoms and Quiggin had already seen her seven or eight times during the past 12 months. He knew that she had seven watertight bulkheads, the forward one watertight to the spar deck in case of collision. She was treble riveted, quadruple riveted in places of great strain, and in all the time he had known her, he had never seen a leaky rivet or any leakage in the upper deck.

The sternpost was strong, much stronger than usual, thought Quiggin, and the stern frame was a solid forging. The bosses to receive the rudder plate were all solid forgings, as was the rudder itself, and the way in which the builders had contrived the tail shaft passing through the stern tube and entering the boss of the propeller was absolutely watertight. "It is the best job I have ever seen," remarked Quiggin, "and I am a shipbuilder myself."

The *Atlantic's* iron masts also came within his jurisdiction and he found that the masts themselves, the yards and the rigging were complete, and that the ship had sails and spare sails according to the Act. She could be steered either from amidships or aft, and Quiggin noticed particularly that the ship's three compasses were as well placed as could be. The 10 lifeboats, all in good order, offered 5,778 cub ft of accommodation, although the act called for only 3,600 cub ft for a ship such as the *Atlantic*. Quiggin had looked at those boats many times and thought they would probably carry up to 60 persons each.

He calculated that their total displacement would be 82 tons and that deducting 42 tons for the weight of the boats themselves gave a total available carrying power of 40 tons or 600 persons each weighing 150 lb. As there were nearly 1,000 persons on board the *Atlantic* on her last voyage, even Quiggin's optimistic calculations left a lot to be desired, but it was widely held that no ship could possibly carry sufficient lifeboats to take off all her passengers and crew. The Passengers Acts of 1855 and 1863 laid down a scale of boats according to the tonnage of the ship, up to one of 1,500 gross tons which had to carry seven lifeboats. The *Atlantic*, more than twice this tonnage, still need only have carried seven lifeboats and it was Ismay's fanatical regard for safety that placed more on board than the law demanded. The same applied to other items of life-saving equipment. All Quiggin and Mylchreest could insist upon were four lifebuoys and six lifebelts, but the *Atlantic* carried many more.

All this was on a par with what the surveyors knew of White Star liners. Neither of them had ever sailed in one, but they talked with the masters and officers, and knew from what they said that they were seakindly vessels. They had no hesitation in giving the *Atlantic* a favourable report; talking about her after she had been lost, Quiggin said, almost with wonder; "She was one of the best built and strongest ships I have ever seen—a thoroughly good ship."

This was an opinion supported by William Cress Taylor, the principal surveyor for the Board of Trade at Liverpool. Taylor spent three-quarters of an hour walking round the ship while she was in drydock, and although he did not go aboard or make a close examination of her, this already having been done by Quiggin and Mylchreest, he found her general condition to be very good. "I found the vessel in good order; in excellent order," he said afterwards. "I cannot say more."

The *Atlantic* was granted a passenger certificate on the strength of Taylor's endorsement of Quiggin's and Mylchreest's report, and on her return from her 17th voyage, in February, 1873, she was seen again by another surveyor, this time William Henry Bisset. Bisset had spent 28 years looking after ships, surveying them, fitting them out and at times sailing in them in different capacities.

He joined the Board of Trade in 1868 and was qualified as a surveyor of both a ship's hull and her engines. Before going to Liverpool he had been surveyor for the Belfast district and had seen the *Atlantic* just after she had been completed by Harland & Wolff. When he saw her again in February, 1873, she was afloat in the West Waterloo Dock, Liverpool, and he formed the opinion that she was just as good then as she had been when she was new. Asked to put his opinion in words, he said: "I think she was one of the most substantial ships that ever entered the port of Liverpool. The whole fleet are on the same principle."

The *Atlantic's* compasses had been adjusted by Thomas Bassnett, of Liverpool, when she was completed at Belfast, and were tested again on February 13, 1873, when she was lying in the Mersey. On the following day she sailed on her 18th voyage to New York, returning on Thursday, March 13. In the previous September, the Mersey Docks and

The Coal was there for Burning

Harbour Board had allocated the White Star Line an area of 2,772 square yards at the West Waterloo Dock as a permanent berth, and it was to this dock that the *Atlantic* went to start preparing for her 19th—and last—crossing of the Western Ocean.

By far the biggest task involved in this preparation was the loading of an adequate supply of coal to take her to New York. One of the first visitors on board was the White Star Line's superintendent engineer, Stewart Gordon Horsburgh, his task being to check on the amount of coal which remained in the bunkers. Horsburgh estimated that there was 160 tons left but the ship's chief engineer reported 132 tons in his log book and Horsburgh agreed to accept this figure. When he left the ship to return to the White Star Line office he took this log with him, and on arriving at the office made out an order for Richards, Power & Co. to supply the ship with approximately 860 tons of mixed Lancashire and South Wales coal.

The South Wales coal came from a mine at Aberdare and totalled 641 tons, 17 cwts, as weighed by the Great Western Railway Co. The Lancashire coal came from the Crow Orchard Colliery at Skelmersdale and weighed 221 tons, 5 cwts, at the minehead. Sixty railway wagons were used to carry the South Wales coal to Birkenhead and just half that number to take the Lancashire coal to the Bramley Moore Dock at Liverpool. In both places, the coal was tipped into lighters for carriage to the *Atlantic*, but one lighter, the *Mary Jane*, was diverted and discharged 16 tons into the White Star Line's tender, the *Traffic*, so that out of the 863 tons, 2 cwts, allocated to the liner she received 847 tons, 2 cwts. For accounting purposes, the odd 2 cwts were ignored.

The loading of the coal was the responsibility of Edward Bozlen, a stevedore employed under contract by the White Star Line. Bozlen's coal stower, Francis M'Kenna, went aboard the ship on the following Sunday to inspect the state of the bunkers, and estimated that they contained about 130 to 140 tons of coal. The chief engineer, recalling that he had entered 132 tons in his log and deducting the amount consumed by the ship during her four days in port, said that according to his figures the amount was 120 tons. This was near enough for M'Kenna and he gave instructions for the lighters to start coming alongside.

Loading started shortly after Sunday midnight, and although the amount was rather more than the capacity of the *Atlantic's* bunkers she had a moveable bulkhead in No. 3 hold, forward of the engine-room, which allowed an amount of coal, depending on the position of the bulkhead, to be carried in the hold. She had, in fact, crossed the Atlantic with as much as 1,470 tons on board and as little as 902 tons. When she sailed on her last voyage, Bozlen, M'Kenna and Horsburgh all estimated that with the moveable bulkhead positioned as it was, she was filled to within about 30 tons of her maximum capacity.

There had also to be placed on board sufficient food and provisions for the *Atlantic's* passengers and crew—such items as 11,016 lb of flour, 4,560 lb of beef, 288 lb of tea, 70 lb of mustard, 1,596 lb of butter, 72 tins of soup, 256 pints of milk, seven gallons of brandy, and seven dozen quarts of port wine. Liverpool Corporation Waterworks supplied 9,400 gallons of fresh water and, in addition, Bisset issued a certificate stating that the *Atlantic's* condensing apparatus had been tested and found capable of supplying 800 gallons of fresh water per day of 12 hours.

The food and water was inspected by Dr. William Spooner, the medical officer at Liverpool responsible to the Board of Emigration Commissioners for seeing that the emigrants were carried in clean, well ventilated conditions and that the provisions supplied for their use were of good quality. Accompanied by Adolphus Large, the White Star Line's shore steward, Dr. Spooner opened some of the provisions at random, to ensure that the food was of the specified quality and that the barrels and boxes were in fact full. He also tested the water, examined the medicine chest and surgical instruments, and satisfied himself that the ship's five hospitals were clean and adequately fitted.

Another visitor on board was William Cunningham Lang, a consulting engineer retained by the White Star Line to advise them on engineering matters. Lang had served in the Merchant Navy and the Royal Navy as an engineer and before setting up in business for himself had been for 11 years superintendent engineer of the West India & Pacific Co. On board the *Atlantic* he examined the machinery and inspected the boiler tubes. He found there was a little scale in the boilers, but apart from that he pronounced the engines to be in good condition.

At the same time, a boilermaker attended to a slack rivet which had allowed water to seep into the forward bunker during the previous voyage. The leak was so trivial, however, that no mention of it was made to the Board of Trade surveyors.

While all this was going on, the *Atlantic* was loading her cargo for New York—earthenware, machinery, beer and miscellaneous items valued at nearly £50,000 and weighing some 768 tons, about 200 tons of which was copper dross put aboard as ballast. Cargo also came within the scope of the Board of Emigration Commissioners and their stowage officer at Liverpool, Robert William Evatt, supervised the loading of the *Atlantic*. Evatt had served in command of ships for 15 years and knew as well as anyone the potential danger of badly stowed cargo; he was satisfied that nothing on board the *Atlantic* constituted a hazard to the ship and neither was it stowed in such a way as to impose a strain upon her hull.

The *Atlantic* moved out of West Waterloo Dock on March 18 and anchored in the River Mersey off Princes Landing Stage, waiting for the last of her coal to arrive. Wednesday, the 19th, passed in a flurry of last minute preparations and on Thursday, March 20, the crew signed on for the Atlantic voyage. Some 23 years earlier, the Liverpool Sailors' Home had been opened, and among its amenities was an office for the engagement and discharge of crews. The system devised by the governors of the Sailors' Home was later adopted by the Board of Trade, and officials of the Home were appointed by the Board to carry out the provisions of the Mercantile Marine Acts relating to the engagement and discharge of seamen. It was to the Sailors' Home in Canning Place, therefore, that the crew of the *Atlantic* went to sign their articles of agreement with the master, Captain James Agnew Williams, a Welshman by some accounts and by others a native of Cork, who was then living at Bootle, near Liverpool.

Captain Williams held a certificate of competency as an extra master, the highest qualification possible for him to obtain in his chosen profession. Long exposure to North Atlantic weather on an open bridge made him look older than his 33 years; he was, by the standard of the time, a young man to be in command of a North Atlantic passenger liner, but his promotion had been rapid. After serving in a number of ships as a junior officer he came ashore in 1865 to study for, and obtain, his master's certificate. He then joined the National Steamship Co. as first officer of the *Pennsylvania*, but left them in the following year to take up a position as master in the Williams & Guion Line's *Nevada, Colorado* and *Wisconsin* but was dismissed in 1871 after a complaint had been made to the company by a passenger who had once been master of a whaler. Despite being pressed after the *Atlantic* disaster to state the nature of this complaint, Stephen Guion would only reply: "The poor man will have trouble enough without bringing that up against him."

The New York press, however, were firmly convinced that Captain Williams had been dismissed due to hazarding his ship, in the whaling master's opinion, because of drunkenness. Be that as it may, Captain Williams left the Guion Line with an excellent reference from Mr. Guion and had no trouble in joining the White Star Line. Defending himself after the disaster Captain Williams stoutly averred: "I promised Thomas Ismay that not a drop of liquor should cross my lips on his vessel and I never broke that promise."

The Coal was there for Burning

Captain Williams was first appointed to the *Republic* and an incident aboard that ship in February, 1872, brought him to the early attention of the management. It was described in a letter from the master of the *Republic*, Captain Digby Murray.

"Since leaving Liverpool," wrote Captain Murray, "we have had nothing but bad weather. We encountered a terrific gale in about lat. 47°, and long. 42° W., our decks were swept, all boats but two entirely destroyed, one of the two left opened right out, the engine-room skylight smashed and driven down on top of the cylinders; this skylight had never been properly bolted or secured.

"Mr. Williams, the second officer, whose pluck and endurance has been beyond all praise, while securing a sail over the fiddley (the engine-room skylight), great quantities of water having gone down and put out the lee fires, was caught by No. 4 boat as it was dashed a perfect wreck inboard, one of the davits unshipping and coming with it, and crushed against the railing round the funnel; his left thigh broke a little above the knee; his left ankle was dislocated; we fear some of his ribs broke."

A passenger in the ship was tremendously impressed. "It was another proof of the force of the sea," he said, "a further explanation of the meaning of 'being struck'; the man was literally crushed; the blood flowed from his ears, mouth and nostrils, his thigh was broken in two places, and his ribs crushed on one side. A powerful man weighing over 200 lb, crushed like an insect by the sea."

"We trust the accident may not prove fatal," Captain Murray continued, "but time only will tell us; he shows amazing pluck, and is at present doing well; if he does not recover, he will be a *very great* loss to the company, for men like him are very few and far between."

Captain Murray was appointed commodore of the White Star Line in March, 1871, and commanded every ship in the company's fleet, including the *Atlantic* for two voyages. He left the company in February, 1873, to join the Board of Trade as their professional adviser, an appointment created under the Mercantile Marine Act of 1850 in order that civil servants might have available the advice of professional seamen on technical matters. He was later created a baronet in recognition of his outstanding service.

On seafaring matters, and as a judge of men, Ismay respected Murray probably more than anybody else, and his letter was sufficient to ensure speedy promotion for Second Officer Williams. As soon as he had recovered from his injuries he was promoted to chief Officer of the *Celtic*, a slightly larger ship than the *Atlantic*, which had just joined the fleet from Harland & Wolff's yard. After only three voyages in the *Celtic* he was appointed master of the *Atlantic* and had already made a complete voyage in her.

Even more so then than now, the master was responsible for anything and everything appertaining to the ship, whether it came within his personal knowledge or not. Thus one of Captain Williams' duties before the ship sailed was to sign an all-embracing declaration which read: "I hereby certify that I have actually on board the steamship *Atlantic* for the use of the passengers, amounting in all to 700 statute adults, the full quantities of provisions and water stipulated by the Passengers Acts 1854 and 1867, as well as a sufficiency of fuel, surgical instruments, medicines, and medical comforts, for the voyage; that I am satisfied with the accommodation for the passengers, as regards the size, stability, and arrangement of the berths; and that the ship is in all respects seaworthy; and that there is not on board, as cargo, any article specified in Sec. 29 likely to endanger the safety of the ship, or the health or lives of the passengers; all of which I attest, with a due sense of the personal responsibility it involves."

Captain Williams' second-in-command was John William Firth, another experienced seaman. Firth held a certificate of competency as master and had sailed in command of the steamer *Iona*, owned by the Anglo-Egyptian Line, but the North Atlantic passenger liners were the crack ships, and Firth decided it was worth taking a drop in rank in order to go to a trans-Atlantic liner company. He had served at sea for 27 years when he joined the White Star Line in 1873 as chief officer of the *Republic*. He had made one voyage in that ship and this was to be his first in the *Atlantic*.

The second officer, Henry Ismay Metcalfe, had come down in rank for a different reason. While serving as chief officer of the steamer *Explorer* in April, 1869, he had been officer-of-the-watch when that ship had collided with and sunk the steamer *Bretagne*. A court of inquiry in Melbourne had found him guilty of neglect of duty and his certificate as mate had been suspended for 12 months, from July, 1869, until June, 1870. When his certificate was restored, Metcalfe went back to sea, joined the White Star Line, and qualified as master in February, 1872. It was his misfortune—perhaps everybody's misfortune—that he was to be senior officer-of-the-watch as the *Atlantic* closed the coast of Nova Scotia on her last voyage.

These three, master, mate and second mate, were all the navigating officers that the *Atlantic* was required by law to carry, but in fact she carried two more. Cornelius Lawrence Brady, the third officer, had served at sea for 20 years and, like Firth, he too held a master's certificate and had commanded his own ship. John Brown, fourth officer, had only been at sea for 10 years, but like the others he was a fully qualified master mariner.

While the *Atlantic* was at sea, two of these officers were always on watch, the chief officer and the third officer together and the second officer and fourth officer together, each pair working four hours on, four hours off, with the exception of the watch from 4 p.m. to 8 p.m. which was split into two periods of two hours each—the dog watches. These served two purposes; they broke the sequence of watches, so that the same pair did not keep the same watch every day, and they provided a more even distribution of time off for the watch below. But for the dog watches, one watch would have had only four hours off every night while the other watch had eight hours off.

Signing on to take charge of the *Atlantic's* engine-room was John Foxley, who probably knew more about the practical working of her machinery than anyone else. He first joined her as third engineer on her third voyage, became second engineer on her seventh voyage, and chief engineer on her 18th voyage. All told, he had been a marine engineer for 18 years and held a first-class certificate of competency issued by the Board of Trade. Under him, in order of seniority, he had three qualified engineers, Robert Ewing, John Hodgson and William Paterson. Each of these kept watch in the engine-room accompanied by a junior engineer, Peter Urquhart, Samuel Davis and Robert MacFarlane. Unlike the deck officers, the engineers did not keep watch and watch but divided into three watches, four hours on and eight hours off, each pair keeping the same watch in each successive period of 12 hours.

The sequence of watches before the stranding was as follows:

March 31

Watch	Deck	Engine-room
Middle watch	Firth	Paterson
Midnight to 4 a.m.	Brady	Urquhart
Morning watch	Metcalfe	Ewing
4 a.m. to 8 a.m.	Brown	MacFarlane
Forenoon watch	Firth	Hodgson
8 a.m. to noon	Brady	Davis

Afternoon watch	Metcalfe	Paterson
Noon to 4 p.m.	Brown	Urquhart
First dog watch	Firth	
4 p.m. to 6 p.m.	Brady	Ewing
		MacFarlane
Second dog watch	Metcalfe	
6 p.m. to 8 p.m.	Brown	
First watch	Firth	Hodgson
8 p.m. to midnight	Brady	Davis

April 1

Middle watch	Metcalfe	Paterson
Midnight to 3·15 p.m.	Brown	Urquhart

Captain Williams and Chief Engineer Foxley did not keep a watch but were always available in case their advice or assistance was needed. Other non-watchkeeping officers were the surgeon, Dr. Thomas Cuppage, and the purser, Ambrose Worthington, their duties being concerned particularly with the emigrants. The senior ratings consisted of two carpenters, two boatswains, six quartermasters, a ship's cook and a ship's steward. Serving under the petty officers were 33 able seamen, 33 engine-room hands, six passengers' cooks, 42 passengers' stewards and three stewardesses. All the crew were adults; there were no ordinary seamen, apprentices or boys. Their grand total, including the master, was 143.

While the crew were signing the articles, and agreeing to undertake the Atlantic crossing for an average wage of £5 per month, the passengers were being ferried out to the ship in the tender *Traffic*. Waiting for them at the top of the gangway were Purser Worthington, to inspect their tickets, and Dr. Cuppage and Dr. Spooner, to inspect their health. In common with other trans-Atlantic companies carrying emigrants, the White Star Line reserved the right to reject passengers who were found to be "lunatic, idiot, deaf, dumb, blind, maimed, infirm or above the age of 60 years . . . or any person unable to take care of himself (or herself) without becoming a public charge." Also likely to be excluded were widows with children or a mother travelling with children but without her husband, the ban being imposed not so much by the shipping company as by the United States Government which refused to allow such persons to land and forced the shipping company to take them back to Europe.

It was also Dr. Spooner's duty, as port medical officer, to detect any kind of infectious disease as the passengers filed past him. If any appeared to be suffering from such a disease he would draw them to one side, with members of their immediate family, in order to examine them more carefully and, if the nature of the disease warranted it, have them put ashore. On this occasion, all the passengers had a clean bill of health.

There were, all told, 27 adults and one child in the first-class accommodation, most of them Americans returning home, and 499 adults, 69 children and 19 babies in the steerage, making 615 in all and, with the crew, a grand total of 758 known to be on board when the ship left Liverpool. A large proportion of the emigrants came from Continental Europe; to them, the *Atlantic* was the last stage in a journey which would carry them from the poverty and misery and oppression of the Old World to the bright hope of health and prosperity held out by the New. Most of them were men whose families would follow when they themselves had found somewhere to settle and had become established, but there was also 167 women travelling with their husbands.

In addition to their luggage, each emigrant possessed the minimum requirements laid down by the company—plate, mug, knife, fork, spoon, water-can and bedding. Once aboard the *Atlantic* they were carefully segregated, married couples, familes and single women, if any, aft; single men forward. During the voyage they would be allowed six pints of water each every day, and as much food as they could eat, cooked and served by the ship's staff.

There was now very little left to be done, but before the ship could be allowed to sail there had to be a final inspection. Captain William Charles Geary, 45 years in the Royal Navy and the Merchant Navy and now an assistant emigration officer, Captain Leonard Spear, the White Star Line's marine superintendent, and Captain Williams, toured the steerage accommodation before the passengers were allowed to go below. This inspection, which lasted half an hour and was completed to the satisfaction of all three, was followed by a muster of the crew. They were, thought Captain Geary, a fair average bunch of men, and seemed to know their work. Certainly during the lifeboat drill which followed the muster, they put up a good show, swinging out two of the ship's boats within four minutes.

Next a careful search was made by the ship's officers for stowaways, but none were discovered. The draft was taken, and found to be 19 ft 8 in forward and 23 ft 7 in aft, giving a mean freeboard of 13 ft 9 in. Now only one thing remained, and Captain Williams was duly served with his clearance certificate. "We, the undersigned surveyors," it read, "duly appointed under and for the purpose of the Passengers Act, in pursuance of directions received from the Emigration Officer at this port, have carefully supervised the above-mentioned steamship, her tackle and equipments; and from such survey . . . we are enabled to report that the above-mentioned ship is, in our opinion, strong, seaworthy and fit in all respects for her intended service, namely, the carriage of passengers to New York."

It was signed by Mylchreest and Quiggin, as Government surveyors for the port of Liverpool, and approved by Commander W. C. Reeves, R.N., the chief emigration officer. Now there was nothing to hold the *Atlantic* back, and shortly after three o'clock in the afternoon of Thursday, March 20, 1873, she weighed anchor and sailed down the River Mersey on her last voyage.

Chapter Four

"Bear up for Halifax!"

IN accordance with company orders, Captain Williams shaped a course from Liverpool to take him to the northward of the Skerries, outside this group of rocks; *the channel inside,* said the regulations, *being considered too narrow and dangerous to admit of large steamers being navigated through it in perfect safety.* From the Skerries, course was steered for the Stack, and with the Stack abeam, course was next altered for the Saltees lightship, this route being designed to take the ship about four miles south of the track followed by ships inward bound for Liverpool. There was a fresh, easterly breeze, which later moderated to north east, and Captain Williams took advantage of it by ordering the sails to be set. With these to aid the engines the *Atlantic* worked up to 13 knots on the passage across the Irish Sea to Queenstown, arriving there at nine o'clock on the Friday morning.

Waiting to welcome her were four more saloon passengers and 143 adult emigrants, all from in and around Dublin, 20 children and eight babies—making a grand total on board of 933, including crew, excluding stowaways.

While they were climbing aboard, Captain Williams took the opportunity to write a short report to the owners: "The *Atlantic* passed the rock at 2.35 p.m. yesterday, and Roche's Point at 8.45 a.m.; had moderate north-east wind down, with clear weather," he said. "Passengers all well; engines working well; coals better; averaged 40 revolutions down. Will pass Roche's Point outwards about 10.30 a.m."

True to his forecast, Captain Williams sailed from Queenstown at half past ten, having been in the Irish port little more than an hour. Now the passengers could settle down to the voyage ahead, and more than one recorded his impressions of White Star service in glowing terms. Breakfast was at half past eight, lunch at one and dinner at six. "The cooking altogether is nearly perfect," said one passenger, "and the service by the waiters most attentive and accommodating.

"In the intervals, wind and weather permitting, the majority of the passengers sit or promenade on the upper deck, where time goes rapidly in making up sweepstakes on the speed of the ship, which are settled at mid-day, when the speed is posted up, and marked down on the pocket charts*; in watching passing vessels; playing at rope quoits; or helping the youngsters to fly kites."

The *Atlantic's* design called for favourable comment, particularly "the good sense of the builders in abandoning the old-fashioned arrangement of placing the cabins and berths in the stern, abaft the engines and over the screw—an arrangement which converts the ship into a factory of sickness, by subjecting the passengers to the greatest motion, the worst smells and the most excruciating dins."

Ismay's theory was paying off, for this passenger found "the main advantage is the position of the saloon in midships, ahead of the cooking galley and the engines, so that none of the odours, or rather mal-odours, of the cookhouse and the engine-room enter the cabin."

* See endpapers.

18

ap, we gain nearly five hours extra sleep during the passage.ha**of the ship'** which commonly turns the stomach of the passenger long before any storm arises."

Ismay's regard for safety was well publicised and promoted a well founded feeling of security. "The nights, to a sound sleeper like myself." wrote another passenger, "have a novel charm—the clock is put back half an hour at midnight, and thus we gain nearly five hours extra sleep during the passage. I love the lullaby of the waves, which sound like the rustling of the leaves of a mighty forest, and although the glimpse of the moonlight through the port window tempts to wakefulness, it is pleasant to slumber to the music of the ocean, varied only by the sound of the boatswain's pipe, the distant singing of the sailors as they hoist the sails to catch a favouring breeze, the half-hourly ringing of the ship's bells, and the answer of the man on the watch that 'All's well'."

But all was not well. According to company's orders, on the first day out Foxley should have furnished Captain Williams with a report on the amount of coal consumed and the amount remaining, and should have submitted a similar report on each successive day of the voyage. The orders were quite clear: *The commander is required each day to examine and sign the engineer's log book, and shall be responsible for any omission that may occur in the same. The commander is likewise enjoined to pay special attention to the daily consumption and remaining stock of coal.* The exact expenditure should also have been entered on the log slate, from which details of the day's run were transferred to the chief officer's log book, but at the beginning of the voyage, at least, neither Captain Williams nor Foxley paid overmuch attention to the coal consumption.

It averaged, they thought, about 70 tons a day and with that knowledge they were content. The coal was brought out of the bunkers into the stokehold in baskets, and by counting the number of baskets used in a day it was possible to gain a fairly accurate knowledge of the amount of coal consumed. Deducting this figure from the total stock at the outset of the voyage should have given the amount remaining, but Foxley had been an engineer long enough to be able to look into the bunkers and estimate what they contained.

There was no other way of knowing exactly what amount there was on board, for while the new stock might have been weighed accurately at the colliery or by the railway company which carried it, the accuracy of the amount put down as being the coal remaining from the previous voyage depended on the estimating ability of the engineer who judged it.

As the engineers were very often right in their estimates, give or take 10 tons or so either way, and as running short of coal was not considered a particularly heinous offence anyway, no one had given any great thought to the problem, although a Captain A. S. Harrison, of Hackney, claimed that "Archimedes screaming his *eureka* through the streets solved the problem; the rest is a mere matter of day-book and arithmetic tables, and clockwork."

Captain Harrison wanted ships to be fitted with $5\frac{1}{4}$ in or larger copper inlet pipes at 30 ft intervals along the keel. Water entering these pipes would be led to a chamber some 10 ft below the waterline. "You will then have on the sides of this chamber." he said, "a pressure of 10 ft more or less. You have thus a pressure of, say, five pounds to the square inch, about, to move an index mechanism that will show the immersion."

19

The Coal was there for Burning

Captain Harrison suggested that the apparatus should be fitted with a dial "like that of an aneroid barometer" on which the displacement could be read, the actual weight on board being read from a table of immersions calculated "to the greatest nicety in the builders' drawing office".

Theoretically, a biscuit cannot be thrown to a seagull without affecting the displacement of a ship; in practice, Captain Harrison would have been satisfied to get within 10 tons in a 3,000-ton ship, but Foxley did not even have the benefit of a practical example of Archimedes' Principle and had to rely on his own judgement.

Sunday, March 23, was a fine day and divine service was held on board the *Atlantic*, followed at noon by lifeboat drill for the crew. That was the last fine day they were to have for a week, for on the Monday, the wind started to freshen and by Tuesday it was blowing a full gale from the south-west.

To Captain Williams it must have brought back painful memories of the *Republic* and the accident which still caused him to limp; one of the *Atlantic's* wheelhouse windows was smashed, No. 10 lifeboat was damaged and No. 4 boat was stove in and rendered unseaworthy. The steering gear was also affected and for a time the hand gear had to be used, but this breakdown was corrected and the *Atlantic* pressed on, with the wind shifting to west-south-west—dead ahead. Her speed was now reduced from the 14 knots she had been making the first day out from Queenstown to eight knots on Tuesday and less than five knots on Wednesday.

Thursday she did a little better, reaching 10 knots, but when the position was calculated at noon on Friday it was found she had dropped back to under eight, and now Captain Williams had something else to worry him. He instructed Firth to find out from the engine-room exactly how much coal was left.

Foxley's log formed, as it were, the pages of a current account, the "coal remaining" at the end of one voyage appearing as "old stock" at the start of the next. The "coal remaining" from the 18th voyage had been 132 tons, and it was this figure which he used in his calculations, adding to it the 847 tons of new coal, to make a total of 979 tons. From this had to be deducted the coal consumed. They had been seven days in Liverpool and the donkey boiler consumed about six tons a day, he reckoned; that was 42 tons. Then there was getting up steam to enter the river and keeping steam on the main engines to stem the tide; say 38 tons, making a round total of 80 tons used before sailing.

Foxley, like any engineer estimating coal, always dealt in round numbers. They were now eight days out and the consumption was 70 tons a day—that made 560 tons, but the donkey boiler had been used in conjunction with the main boilers for four days. That would burn, say, five tons a day or another 20 tons, making a total of 580 tons. Foxley's scribbling pad when he had finished these calculations looked something like this:

Old stock	132 tons
New stock	847 tons
	979 tons
Consumed in port	80 tons
3 p.m. March 20 to noon 21st	70 tons
To noon 22nd; main and donkey	75 tons
To noon 23rd; main and donkey	75 tons
To noon 24th; main and donkey	75 tons

20

To noon 25th; main and donkey............................	75 tons
To noon 26th; main only.....................................	70 tons
To noon 27th; main only.....................................	70 tons
To noon 28th; main only.....................................	70 tons
	————
	660 tons
On board...	979 tons
Consumed..	660 tons
	————
Remaining	319 tons
	————

Foxley wrote this figure of 319 tons on a slip of paper and gave it to his steward to take to the master.

Captain Williams placed it in a clip in the wheelhouse and let the *Atlantic* run for another day, but at noon on Saturday, the 29th, with no sign of a real improvement in the weather, although the wind had moderated a little, he gave orders to the engine-room to be as careful as they could with the coal, and to the chief steward to let the galley fires go as low as possible, and to put them out as soon as he could. With the wind reduced the sails were set but another gale blew up on the Sunday, the foresail carried away entirely and the fore staysail and fore trysail were split. That day, Foxley confided to the chief officer that although he had got the consumption down to 65 tons, perhaps even 60 tons, he was worried about the coal position.

Captain Williams was also becoming worried, very worried indeed. No White Star ship had ever before had to divert from her voyage because of lack of coal, although it was a frequent happening in other lines, but for the first time he began to think seriously of the possibility of putting in to Halifax.

Monday morning dawned with all the promise of a fine day, with a light head wind and a moderate south-westerly swell, but Captain Williams was not in a mood to enjoy the weather. At eight o'clock he told Foxley to give him a report that was as accurate as possible on the amount of coal that was left; not to stand on his own judgement but to send the other engineer officers as well into the bunkers so that an average based on all their experience might be obtained. Foxley agreed that this was a wise course to adopt, but he also set out on a fresh round of calculations, because the figure produced that day would have to agree with what he had entered in his log book on previous days.

He had already given a total remaining of 319 tons. They had then gone another 24 hours at full consumption, 70 tons, and two days at a reduced consumption of possibly 60 tons—a deduction of 190 tons.

His figures now looked like this:

Consumed in port..	80 tons
3 p.m. March 20 to noon 21st.............................	70 tons
To noon 22nd; main and donkey...........................	75 tons
To noon 23rd; main and donkey	75 tons
To noon 24th; main and donkey...........................	75 tons
To noon 25th; main and donkey...........................	75 tons
To noon 26th; main only.....................................	70 tons
To noon 27th; main only.....................................	70 tons

The Coal was there for Burning

To noon 28th; main only..	70 tons
To noon 29th; main only..	70 tons
To noon 30th; main only..	60 tons
To noon 31st; main only	60 tons
	—————
	850 tons
Coal remaining...	129 tons
	—————
	979 tons
	—————

Ewen said there were between 150 and 160 tons in the bunkers, Hodgson said 160 tons, Paterson said 150 tons—and Foxley agreed with them. It looked to him like the amount of coal the *Atlantic* would burn in two days' steaming, and still leave a bit over. But he knew what the reaction would be if he gave Captain Williams a chit saying there was two days' coal—140 tons—in the ship.

He could almost hear him saying it. "Where's this other lot come from?" he would ask. "Have we been worrying for nothing, Mr. Foxley, because you can't add up properly?"

It was there right enough, in the bunkers, thought Foxley, though for the life of him he could not understand how his calculations and visual estimate could be so far apart. But despite the disbelief in his mind, he was not going to lay himself open to ridicule. With the mental reservation that there was at least two days' steaming in the bunkers, he wrote out a slip for Captain Williams saying there were 129 tons of coal left in the ship.

The forenoon watch that day, from eight o'clock to noon, was taken by the chief officer and the third officer, Firth and Brady. Shortly before noon they were joined on the bridge by Captain Williams, and all three took a careful sextant observation in order to ascertain their position. It worked out to be latitude 41°39′ N, long. 63°54′ W.

Captain Williams turned to the third officer: "Go down to the chief engineer," he said, "and ask him to bring me the exact figure of coal remaining in the ship."

Brady went below to Foxley's room, leaving the chief officer to keep watch on deck while Captain Williams went to the chartroom to lay the position on the chart. Within a few minutes, his message delivered, Brady returned on deck to await the second officer who would relieve him as soon as he had had his lunch.

Sailing ships were navigated from the quarterdeck, the portion of the upper deck from the mainmast to right aft, from which the officer-of-the-watch had a reasonable view forward and could keep an eye on the sails while remaining close to the man at the wheel.

With the introduction of paddle steamers a bridge was built across the ship linking the paddle boxes, and when the screw propeller replaced the paddle wheel the bridge was retained as a raised lookout position.

This was all the bridge consisted of in the *Atlantic*; a railed-off section above the forward end of the upper deck, without any form of covering and containing no navigational equipment, its prime purpose being to provide the officer-of-the-watch with an observation platform. In a modern ship, the bridge is the control centre and incorporates both the wheelhouse and the chartroom and often the wireless-room as well, but in the *Atlantic* the wheelhouse, containing the engine-room telegraph, and the chartroom were on the deck below and about 30 ft aft of the bridge.

It was to this chartroom that Foxley took his slip of paper bearing the coal figure, but Captain Williams barely glanced at it.

"129 tons, is it?" he asked.

22

Foxley agreed that it was. "It's two days' steaming", he muttered, but Captain Williams had already turned back to the chart and did not hear. At least, he did not acknowledge the significance of the remark and Foxley did not press the point.

Captain Williams in fact was no longer interested in the engineer. Instead, he sought the opinion of the only other officer now capable of offering him advice. Firth was an experienced seaman and it was this capable second-in-command whom Captain Williams next called into the chartroom.

"What do you make of that?" he asked, showing him the coal note.

"I don't like it, sir," said Firth frankly. "Not with so many passengers on board."

Turning their backs on the engineer, the two seamen bent over the chart, the tool of their trade and something on which they could rely, although the message it spelled out that day was as irrevocable as it was unpalatable. They were 460 miles from New York—33 hours' steaming if they could make 14 knots, but at the moment they were making only seven. At that speed it would take them nearly two and a half days. Two and a half days' steaming at even 65 tons a day would cost them more than 160 tons of coal. Foxley could have told them there was an even chance of there being 160 tons in the bunkers, but Captain Williams did not see fit to query his estimate, and Foxley saw no reason to volunteer the information.

The barometer was falling, there was the likelihood of another westerly gale blowing up, and if they went on they would either have to be towed ignominiously into New York or, worse, have the ship powerless and drifting on the Nantucket shoals. Captain Williams knew his company's orders: *The commanders must distinctly understand that . . . they must run no risk which might by any possibility result in accident to their ships . . . .*

"What do you think, Mr Foxley?" asked Captain Williams. "We'll be the first ship of the line ever to put into Halifax for coal."

"Better to be sure than sorry," replied Foxley shortly.

All this talk of wind and weather was no concern of his. He had told the master the position and if he thought the weather was against them then that was all there was to it.

To go into Halifax would delay them considerably, thought Captain Williams, but *no supposed gain in expedition, or saving of time on the voyage, is to be purchased at the risk of accident.*

"Very well," he decided. "Bear up for Halifax."

Halifax harbour was—still is—one of the finest in the world, and although the dangers off its entrance called for caution in 1873, it was easier to approach than any other harbour, large or small, on the coast of Novia Scotia. The entrance was marked by three lighthouses. One, on the western side of the 5½-mile-wide entrance, was placed on Chebucto Head and served to guide vessels clear of the dangerous Duncan Reef and Bell Rock, lying southward of Chebucto Head. Another was on Devil's Island on the eastern side of the entrance, and marked Thrum Cap Shoal. The third was on Sambro Island, to the south and west of Chebucto Head. Sambro Island served as a landfall for vessels approaching Halifax from the United States or from the south, as was the *Atlantic*.

The decision having been taken to alter course for Halifax there was nothing to be gained by delay and everything to lose. It was now one o'clock and they were 170 miles from Sambro Island, with every minute taking them nearer to New York and further away from their chance of obtaining fuel. Course was therefore altered to N. 24° E. and, because conserving coal was no longer necessary, the order to economise was countermanded. It was not long before the news spread round the ship that the change had been made, and to one man at least it gave considerable satisfaction.

The Coal was there for Burning

Like the good steward he was, Hugh Christie never missed a chance to replenish his store cupboards. During the gales of the previous week some of his store of potatoes had been deluged with sea water, and the Roman Catholic passengers were complaining of a lack of salt fish. A call at Halifax would give him a heaven sent opportunity to restock with these commodities.

It was a different story in the engineers' mess, where the news was greeted with astonishment by the senior men who had only that morning seen with their own eyes the quantity of coal remaining in the bunkers. Foxley, too, expressed surprise, although he was careful not to mention that his official declaration to the master had been 129 tons. And as it happened, the engineers had something else to talk about, for whatever the amount, it was just as liable to spontaneous combustion as any other coal.

A fire in the bunkers was not unusual; little more than a nuisance really, for lack of oxygen prevented the coal from bursting into flame and more often than not it simply smouldered. But it had to be attended to or it would spread and all the coal would be consumed. As it was, the affected coal would be no use for heating the boilers and its smouldering filled the stokehold with smoke. Hodgson, whose watch it was when the smouldering was first noticed, had put a hosepipe into the bunkers, raked over the coals to make sure they would all be thoroughly wetted, and had had the business in hand within three-quarters of an hour, at the expense of about three tons of coal.

During the afternoon, both anchors were got out over the bows, the leads made ready and armed, and the leadlines overhauled. By four o'clock, when Firth and Brady went up to the bridge for the first watch, the *Atlantic* was making 11 knots in fine weather, but the storm which had been threatening all day was closing in and by the time they were relieved at six by Metcalfe and Brown it was raining heavily. No advantage could be gained from the wind, which was shifting between south-east and south-west, and the sails were furled and the yards squared up.

Firth and Brady took over the watch again at eight o'clock and now the wind veered to the west and the weather took a turn for the better, with only occasional clouds blotting out the bright starlight. During the afternoon, Captain Williams had taken several azimuths and had obtained nine degrees easterly deviation. During the early evening, he confirmed this by the Pole Star, so that course was maintained by compass at N. 24° E., with 9° deviation, which Captain Williams considered to be ample allowance for the westerly set, and would eventually lead the ship to a point five miles to the east of Sambro Island.

From where he stood over on the coast, Benjamin Fulker, the lighthouse keeper on Devil's Island, could see the lights sweeping out to sea from both Sambro Island and Chebucto Head. The weather was then fine and clear, but by 10 o'clock it had deteriorated considerably. At Sambro it was blowing hard, south-south-west, raining heavily, and with a strong sea running. Keeper William Gilkie called the Royal Artilleryman who was stationed with him, George Head, to fire two guns as a warning. Fulker noticed that he could no longer see the Sambro light.

On the *Atlantic*, first-class passenger Daniel Kennane found the night comfortable enough to stroll on deck. There was a light breeze and he enjoyed watching the stars which occasionally became visible through the overcast. At half past ten he was joined by another passenger J. Spencer Jones, who had embarked at Queenstown, and together they went to the smoke-room, where they discussed the ship's change of course with Captain Williams. They parted at 11 o'clock, the passengers to their beds, the master to give instructions to his steward to bring him a cup of cocoa at twenty minutes to three in the chartroom, where he intended spending the night.

"Bear up for Halifax!"

At 11 o'clock, Edward Johnston, lighthouse keeper at Chebucto Head, noticed that Sambro Light was obscured by heavy rain, but for Chief Officer Firth on the bridge of the *Atlantic* the last of the dark clouds had passed over and the ship was in clear weather.

The log to be regularly hove, and the ship's position to be ascertained . . . .

As was his practice, Captain Williams went up to the bridge at ten to twelve to leave his night orders, but before doing so he instructed Brady to work out the distance the ship had run from the change of course at one o'clock until midnight.

Brady had just completed his rounds of the ship preparatory to handing over to his relief and the additional task did not take him very long.

Although the *Atlantic* was fitted with Massey's patent log it was seldom used, and instead the common log was hove every two hours. This consisted of a line marked at regular intervals, the first three marks being one, two and then three strips of leather, the fourth a piece of cord with two knots in it, the fifth a piece of cord with a single knot, the sixth three knots, the seventh a single knot and the eighth four knots, and so on.

To the end of the line was attached the log chip, a triangular piece of wood weighted at one end so as to float upright in the water. When thrown overboard the log chip would remain more or less stationary in the water while the ship sailed away from it, the log line being paid out accordingly for a set time, measured by a sand glass. The intervals between the marks on the line bore the same proportion to the nautical mile as did the time the sand took to run through the glass to the seconds in an hour. The marks on a standard log line were 47 ft 3 in apart, and required a 28-second glass, but if the ship was doing more than about 10 knots a 14-second glass was used, and the result doubled.

This was the device used to measure the *Atlantic's* speed, and Brady calculated that at midnight she was making something like 12 knots, that is, 12 nautical miles per hour. Over a period of 11 hours this would have given a distance of 132 miles but from his previous reckonings, Brady considered that this speed had not been constant. Calculating the distance covered between each cast of the log gave an overal distance of 122 miles, or an average speed of just over 11 knots, and it was this distance which Brady wrote on a slip of paper and gave to Captain Williams.

Captain Williams took it into the chartroom, and shortly afterwards told Firth that he placed the ship a little over 47 miles from Sambro Light.

The commander to enter in the night order-book the course to be steered, and all other necessary instructions.

Captain Williams' orders were concise; To keep a good lookout for ice—that was standard in these waters; to look out for Sambro Light, and if it were seen to get it at least two points on the port bow, and call him immediately; in any circumstances to call him not later than three o'clock, it being his intention to heave to at that time and wait for daylight.

. . . a cautious, prudent and ever watchful system of navigation, which shall lose time or suffer any other temporary inconvenience rather than run the slightest risk which can be avoided.

Eight bells—midnight—and a change of watch. On the bridge, Metcalfe and Brown took over from Firth and Brady; in the engine-room, Paterson and Urquhart came on duty to find the fires low and 36 lb pressure on the steam gauge, and immediately started the black gang stoking up. Captain Williams took a final look round, a final check on the course, a final run over his orders, and then walked the 30 ft aft to the chartroom. On the way he met Brady, who had still not gone below.

"Tell Mr. Brown to give me a shout if the weather thickens," the captain told him.

The Coal was there for Burning

In the chartroom, he prepared to lay down until called by his steward at twenty to three, but he was not to be left in peace. Aboard the *Atlantic* was a journalist, Cyrus M. Fisher, who scented a story in the change of course and wanted the details for his paper, the *Cosmopolitan*. Knowing better than to interrupt the master when he was on duty, he bided his time and boned Captain Williams in the chartroom just as he was preparing to turn in, and managed to keep him from his sleep for 20 minutes while he extracted from him the reason for the diversion.

When he had gone, Captain Williams reviewed the events of the day. It was a sad thing, to be the first ship of the line to have to put in for coal, but it had undoubtedly been the wisest thing to do under the circumstances. As he had done so often before when the ship was at sea, he lay down on the settee in the chartroom, fully clothed and within easy call of the officers-of-the-watch. Within minutes he was fast asleep, unaware that down below, Paterson and his stokers had cleaned the fires, opened the expansion valve, and pushed the pressure up to 54 lb. The *Atlantic*, imperceptibly, began to gather speed.

Midnight was also a time for coffee, preparation of which could only be trusted to the standby quartermaster of the watch. The *Atlantic's* six quartermasters—Roylance, Speakman, Thomas, Owen, Williams and Purdie—were all experienced hands, the best seamen in the ship, picked not only for their competence but for their reliability. They worked watch and watch with the officers, three on duty at a time, one at the wheel, one in the after wheelhouse to attend to the steering engine if necessary and to take over the manual steering gear should the engine fail, and one on standby on the bridge, the standby man's lot being to run errands for the officers, keep lookout as and when required, polish the brasswork when there was nothing else to do—and make coffee. The middle watch started with Williams at the wheel, Roylance aft and Thomas on standby.

Of all the *Atlantic's* navigating officers, only Brady had been to Halifax before, but he did not know the coast particularly well, and only one man felt any misgivings at the way the ship was rushing through the night to an unknown landfall. Quartermaster Thomas knew the coast of Nova Scotia, knew particularly that the land about Sambro Island was low lying, but that to the westward the shore was steep-to and rocky, bounded by high white cliffs. There were numerous off-shore islands, outcroppings of the Sambro Ledges, and the only place of any note, the port of Prospect at the mouth of the Prospect River, offered no harbour of refuge for a ship the size of the *Atlantic*.

When Thomas had been called for the middle watch by Quartermaster Purdie he asked whether Sambro Light had been sighted.

"No, not yet," Purdie replied. "She hasn't run the distance."

"We have," said Thomas, "I'm sure we have. We ought to be seeing the light now."

Thomas had made a note of the ship's position at one o'clock and had gone to the trouble of finding out the latitude and longitude of Halifax, not from one of the ship's officers but from a gazetteer owned by a passenger. According to his calculations, unqualified navigator though he was, the ship was very close to the land. These thoughts were in his mind as he went through the routine of the standby quartermaster. Taking the kettle from the wheelhouse, he went down to the stokehold for boiling water, brewed a pot of coffee, and returned to the bridge, where he poured it out for Metcalfe, Brown and himself. When he had drunk his own he relieved Williams at the wheel so that he might have a drink and then, when Williams took the wheel again, Thomas went aft with the coffee pot to give a drink to Roylance in the steering flat.

Returning again to the bridge, he got out the brass box and began polishing the brightwork until half past one, when Brown called him to assist in casting the log. Thomas's job was to hold the reel while Brown threw the log chip over the side. After allowing a certain length of line—the stray line—to get clear of the propeller wake, Brown called "Turn!" and Metcalfe turned the sandglass. As soon as Metcalfe called "Stop!" Brown tightened his grip on the line and noted from the mark how much had run out. It gave a reading of nine knots, but Thomas felt sure the *Atlantic* was doing more than that, more like $11\frac{1}{2}$ to 12 knots.

Risking the rebuff which he knew must follow, he told the second officer the ship had run far enough, and that they should heave to.

At sea, when the officer-of-the-watch believes the ship to be running into danger, it is his duty to act, at once, upon his own responsibility.

"I am not the captain," replied Metcalfe tartly, "and you are not the mate."

Still uneasy in his mind, Thomas went down to the saloon deck, hearing four bells (two o'clock) strike as he went. Brown was standing on the starboard side of the wheelhouse, and Thomas suggested to him that he should climb to the main yard to look out for land.

"You won't see any," Brown replied. "We haven't run our distance yet."

"You won't feel the land until you strike it," Thomas said, but Brown still refused to let him go aloft.

There was nothing more that Thomas could do, except relieve Williams at the wheel and hold the course that had been ordered. But he was a very worried man, despite the knowledge that Able Seaman Joseph Carroll had been ordered to Stand on No. 1 house, forward of the bridge, with orders to look out for Sambro Light. Thomas would have been happier seeking the light from the higher vantage point of the main yard. From where he stood at the wheel he could see another lookout, Patrick Kiely, posted on the starboard side of the bridge, also looking for the light. Thomas didn't think he'd see anything from there.

There was one other worried soul aboard the *Atlantic*. William Hogan, one of the emigrants, had been lying awake waiting, for no particular reason, for the ship to drop anchor. When he heard five bells strike (half past two) he got up and went on deck. Everything seemed as usual. The night was extremely cold, but the weather was fine, better than it had been earlier. The ship seemed to be running well, and Hogan went back to bed with an easier mind.

Punctually at twenty to three, the captain's steward arrived on deck with a cup of cocoa in his hand.

"Where is the captain, sir?" he asked Brown. "Is he on the bridge?"

"No," Brown told him. "He's asleep in the chartroom."

"I'm supposed to call him," the steward said.

Unlike Fisher, Brown knew how valuable it was for the captain to snatch as much sleep as he could, when he could. Brown's orders, passed on by Brady, were that the master was only to be called if the weather got worse.

"You'd better go and see Mr. Metcalfe," he told the steward. "He'll tell you whether to call him or not."

Still carefully bearing his cup of cocoa, the steward went on up to the bridge and asked Metcalfe if he should call the captain.

"No," ordered the second officer. "I'll call him when it's time to call him."

The ship is never to be left without an officer in charge of the deck.

Brown then set off on one of his regular rounds of the ship, leaving Metcalfe, his senior officer, in charge. From where he stood on the bridge, Metcalfe had no means of telling the time, but he knew it must be near the time when Captain Williams wanted to be roused, and he called out to Thomas at the wheel to tell him what time it was.

Thomas had a clock right in front of him, and told Metcalfe it was twelve minutes past three. Metcalfe thereupon left the bridge, went down to the chartroom and opened the door,

"Captain Williams!" he called. "Quarter past three but no sign of the light!"

The chartroom being immediately adjacent to the wheelhouse, Thomas knew that Captain Williams had not roused from his sleep, and when Metcalfe made as though to walk away, the quartermaster suggested to him that he should go in and make sure that the captain was awake. Thomas was an outspoken man, and this time Metcalfe did as he said, but no sooner had he entered the chartroom than Carroll, from his vantage point on the forward deckhouse saw a streak of white showing through the black night.

"Breakers ahead!" he yelled.

Because icebergs were a more likely hazard both Metcalfe and Thomas thought it was ice he was reporting, and Metcalfe, who had dashed out of the chartroom on hearing the lookout's call, returned to tell Captain Williams that the ship was among ice.

Quartermaster Roylance, in the after wheelhouse, also saw the breakers and ran forward to warn the bridge, and now Kiely, the bridge lookout, joined in the clamour and shouted that there were breakers or ice ahead. Thomas left the wheel and went to the ship's side, followed by Captain Williams and the second mate, but no further confirmation was needed. The *Atlantic* struck at full speed on the Golden Rule Rock, a low-lying reef off Mars Head, on the southernmost point of Mosher Island.

Chapter Five

Shipwreck!

AROUND Sambro Island and along the entire coast to the west of Halifax the sea is thickly sprinkled with sharp, jagged and splintered rocks, most of them under water and thrusting up from the bottom like gigantic spikes. The coast itself presents a dangerous and awe-inspiring appearance, utterly barren and consisting of nothing but desolate rock. The high, frowning headlands and bold, grey, granite shores are penetrated by deep inlets, but everywhere lie the offshore outcrops which are only dignified by the name of island because they are slightly bigger, though no less rugged, than the rocks which surround them. It was into one of these rocks that the *Atlantic* thrust her iron stem, full tilt. She was not far from the little fishing village of Lower Prospect, but she was 20 miles off her course to Halifax.

At the moment of impact Metcalfe ran back into the wheelhouse and swung the engine-room telegraph hard over to "Full astern" while Thomas hurled the spokes of the wheel full round to starboard, but it was too late for action of this sort. With the engines still pounding full ahead, the hull of the ship slammed down four or five times on the unyielding rock, shattering her plates in half a dozen places. Her stern swung round to the eastward and for a moment she lay still, with a slight list to port.

Metcalfe ordered Roylance to call all hands on deck and Roylance ran immediately to the quartermasters' room and burst the door open with his foot. Purdie, Owen and Speakman who were inside asleep were quickly made aware of the situation and Roylance and Speakman got a lamp from the wheelhouse and than ran aft to where the rockets were stored. After firing seven successfully the rocket box rolled away from them and they could fire no more.

Fourth Engineer Paterson had gone down from the control platform to the stokehold and was standing opposite No. 2 boiler when he felt the ship touch the bottom almost directly under his feet, on the starboard side of the keel, as if she were grazing over something. Paterson was surfacing No. 1 starboard boiler and immediately shut the surface cock and ran up to the engine-room. When he got there he saw the telegraph had been thrown round beyond the usual mark for going full astern, as if it had been pulled violently. Urquhart had answered the signal and was in the act of reversing the engines, assisted by a greaser, James Denney. When the engines were going astern Paterson watched the telegraph for half a minute more to see if there were going to be any more orders from the deck, and at the same time saw that the engine-room clock marked 19 minutes past three o'clock. When no more signals came he placed the throttle valve handle in Urquhart's charge while he went below to shut the service sea cocks.

As soon as he got to the foot of the engine-room ladder the engines began to race and he shouted to Urquhart to stop them, but before he could get to the stokehold the engines raced again, and turning about he saw that Foxley had entered the engine-room and was looking after the throttle valve. Foxley stopped the engines and told Urquhart to shut the main stop valve, and then went himself to open the safety valve.

Paterson went on into the stokehold, but found that all the firemen had left. Aware now that the ship was in great danger, and that he had further to go to reach safety than anyone, he went round the stokehold shutting the sea cocks, and had just reached the last when a great gush of water swept out of the starboard after bunkers.

Paterson had about 12 ft to run before reaching the ladder, and by the time he found the bottom rung there was a foot of water over the stokehold floor and rising rapidly. Heaving himself up the ladder he found the engine-room empty and there being nothing more he could do, he made his way to the upper deck.

For many of those on board, the sound of the *Atlantic* grating and grinding on the rocks heralded a surge of water through the hull which carried all before it, taking no account of man, woman or child, emigrant, saloon passenger or sailor. The crew and the unaccompanied male passengers survived, those of them who were quick-witted enough to ignore every other consideration except the need to get out of the confines of the hull and on to the open deck. Women who stopped to dress or reassure their children were overwhelmed as the water rose quickly through the gashes torn in the liner's hull. Men who tried to help their loved ones were themselves helpless, for it was every man for himself and he who dallied was lost. The weak died quickly, including a woman who had given birth to a child only hours before the crash and another whose labour never started and whose child died before it was born. Not only was every woman on board lost and every child except one, but in every instance where there was a married couple, both perished.

William Hogan, who only a short time previously had thought how well the ship was running, had not gone back to sleep and was one of those who heard the lookout give the alarm. At the same instant there was a tremendous crash and a rush of air blew out all the lights. Hogan called out to his sleeping companions that the boiler had burst and that they should rush up on deck, but some of them refused to go, claiming that it was just as well to die down below as out in the open. Hogan and another passenger, Patrick Leahy, were determined to save their lives if it was at all possible and despite the confusion they made their way successfully to the upper deck.

Thomas Walsh, another steerage passenger, thought the shock that woke him was the anchor dropping in Halifax harbour but when the ship made a second plunge he realized she was ashore. The companionway quickly became thronged with passengers but the water was pouring in on them and Walsh urged them to get back to their bunks and cling to the iron stanchions.

Roylance, in the meantime, had gone to help Captain Williams to launch No. 3 lifeboat, and had just got her full of passengers and clear of the chocks when Captain Williams asked if the plugs were in. Roylance replied that they were not, and that with the passengers huddled together and crying in the bottom of the boat it would be difficult to fit them. Captain Williams told him to do his best, and went on to No. 5 lifeboat which Metcalfe was handling.

Third Officer Brady had been thrown from his bunk by the force of the collision and came to his senses to find that Brown, with whom he shared a room almost over the propeller, had locked the door before he went on watch, a precaution intended to keep thieves among the emigrants out of the officers' accommodation. There was another smaller door leading into the after wheelhouse and while Brady was opening this, someone—and Brady never found out who—opened the main door and he was able to get out on deck, still in his nightclothes. Unaware of what had happened, he met Quartermaster Williams and asked him what was the matter.

"My God, sir," the man replied, "the ship is on the shore."

Brady's lifeboat was No. 4, the one which had been stove in during the passage, so he made for No. 5, the captain's boat on the starboard side of the saloon deck, all those to port having been carried away by the seas which were sweeping that side of the ship. Captain Williams and Metcalfe already had some 30 or 40 people in the boat when Captain Williams felt a tremble run through the hull. Fearing that she was going to fall over to starboard, he pulled two women out of the boat and half carried them to a place of safety in the mainmast rigging, at the same time shouting to Metcalfe to do the same with the others. The warning came too late, and with a lurch the *Atlantic* capsized to starboard, crushing the laden lifeboat under her iron sides. When Captain Williams struggled back to the mainmast rigging the women, too, had been swept away.

The ship now lay on her side at an angle of 50°, nearly submerged, and swept continuously by icy seas. Walsh and his friends, still clinging to the stanchions which supported their bunks in the steerage accommodation, now found that their only way out was through the extra large portholes which Ismay had provided for their comfort, never dreaming that one day they would enable passengers to escape death by drowning. The portholes, however, were over their heads and many fell back into the water or drowned entangled in their bunks. Walsh watched twenty or more climb through successfully before he himself escaped. Hogan and Leahy also managed to hold on as the ship went over and, along with many others, climbed into the rigging where, despite the coldness of the wind and the icy spray, they felt reasonably safe.

Hogan recalled this moment particularly. "I then heard a dismal wail which was fearful to listen to," he said. "It proceeded from the steerage passengers below, who were then smothering. It did not last more than two minutes, when all was still as death."

Chief Officer Firth was roused by the shock when the ship struck and went on deck to find a number of men trying to launch the remains of No. 4 lifeboat. It was just clear when a wave came and swept it away. No. 7 lifeboat was then cleared for lowering but the sea was sweeping right over the stern of the ship where this boat was situated and it, also, was lost. When the ship keeled to windward and seaward Firth took refuge in the mizzen rigging, taking up a position which he was to maintain for many hours.

Brady also leaped for the mizzen rigging and found that Quartermaster Owen had joined him there. These two men then made their way forward along the crazily angled deck, passing Captain Williams in the main rigging but, because of the noise of the surf and the screams of those trapped in the hull, they were unable to attract his attention. When he reached the bridge Brady could see the rock rising from the reef which the ship had struck. It seemed to be about 75 ft away and he suggested to Owen that one of them should try to swim to it carrying a rope. Owen said he would go and Brady shouted to Captain Williams to tell him what he intended. This time Captain Williams heard him and called out: "Are there any seamen in the rigging?"

Roylance replied and at Captain Williams' bidding he went aloft by the main topmast rigging to unreeve the signal halyard but the main topsail brace carried away and he had to come down again. Brady, however, had obtained a signal halyard of his own and together he and Owen scrambled down to the deck while Roylance assisted Captain Williams into the forward rigging. Owen lashed the rope to the rail and fastened the other end round his waist. Then he plunged over the side into the maelstrom which foamed between the ship and the rock.

By this time Speakman had climbed to the top of the wheelhouse, where he found that by holding on to the rail and lowering his legs over the end he could haul up any person who cared to hang on to his feet. While he was doing this one of the ship's stewards, Frederick

The Coal was there for Burning

Raby, passed by and shouted that the rock could be seen ahead. Speakman left his self-imposed task and made his way along the ship's side, forward, where he heard someone calling his name. With the spray-filled air now thick with sleet Speakman could not see who it was, but he recognized the voice.

"Are you Mr. Brady?" he called.

"Yes!" Brady shouted back. "Give me a hand!"

Owen was rapidly losing his battle to reach the rock and it took the combined strength of Brady and Speakman to haul him back, exhausted, to the ship. Undaunted, Speakman said he would have a try. Taking off his clothes and donning a lifebelt he tied the rope round his waist and went over the side.

It was a long, hard struggle in the broken water but Speakman eventually reached the rock, to find that its steep sides offered no foothold. Only after swimming for some distance along the face of the rock was he at last able to find a place where he could pull himself ashore. Speakman was not the first to reach the rock, however. Lying there, almost dead, was a sailor from the *Atlantic* but whether he had jumped overboard deliberately or been washed overboard Speakman neither knew nor cared. Kicking him into some semblance of life he ordered him to hold the rope and on no account let it go.

Seeing Speakman climb safely ashore, Brady unrove the fore trysail vang, a practically new rope and heavier and stronger than the signal halyard. Quickly fastening it to the end of the halyard, he signalled to Speakman to haul away. Now with the vang secured to the rock there was established a bridge for those agile and strong enough to use it, and Brady made the first passage, followed by Owen and some of the stronger passengers and members of the crew. Their survival was still by no means assured, for the rock was only 70 ft wide and was being swept continually by waves, but at least their lot seemed preferable to that of those left aboard the ship where, with each successive wave, one or more lost their tenuous hold in the rigging and dropped into the sea. Many had taken the precaution of donning a lifebelt but because, in their haste, they neglected to put them on properly, their feet instead of their heads were kept out of the water.

Quartermaster Thomas had also had a narrow escape when the ship capsized. From the bridge he ran to the after wheelhouse to get some axes, which he distributed to members of the crew so that they could cut away the gear encumbering the lifeboats. While he was doing this he met Mary Money, a widow who was travelling in the steerage with her brother, Alfred, and her small son. Thomas had become friendly with Mrs. Money during the passage and when she pleaded with him to save her and her boy he promised that he would do his best. Thomas took them up on to the saloon deck but when the ship heeled over Mrs. Money and her son lost their grip on the rail despite Thomas's attempt to hold them and he never saw them again.

Quartermaster Purdie held on and catching up with Thomas he suggested that as the distance from the stern to Mosher Island appeared to be less than from the bow to the rock, they should try to swim to the island, but Thomas at first refused. Purdie decided to have a try, but was caught by a heavy breaker and disappeared in the foam. Thomas thought he had been pulled down by the weight of his clothes, so before he set off himself he took off his coat, his guernsey frock and his seaboots. The distance was deceptive for it was actually some 600 ft to the island but Thomas reached it safely and looking back to the ship found that a passenger whose name he never learned had followed him. Helping him ashore they stumbled inland, sometimes falling in the pitch darkness as they searched for assistance.

Back aboard the wreck another three lines had been hauled over to the rock and Captain Williams and Fourth Officer Brown were urging the passengers and crew to avail themselves of the chance of safety which they offered.

32

Shipwreck!

One of those who crossed over was William Hoy, a 24-year-old well-built Irish emigrant from Antrim. Although sailing as a passenger, Hoy was a seaman from a long family of seamen and the traditions of the sea were firmly instilled in him. As soon as he had climbed up the slippery side of the rock he set himself to help those who had not the strength or skill to help themselves. Hoy had already been exposed to the weather for some hours aboard the ship but although only lightly clad and suffering greatly from the cold he lay down in the snow which covered the upper surface of the rock and as the survivors came across on the rope he caught them by their arms, their clothing, their hair—anywhere where he could get a hold—and hauled them up to a place where they could stand. It was hard work and dangerous, for every time he pulled a man up he took the risk of being pulled down himself, but he carried on until his hands became numb and he could use them no longer, but still he did not give up. Leaning even further over the side of the rock he set his teeth into the clothes of the survivors and, by drawing himself back, drew them up as well. The heroic stand of the sailor-passenger at the wreck of the *Atlantic* is still remembered in Islandmagee in the words of a poem by the Hon. Winifred E. Rollo:

> Four hours, says one who saw,
>   In cold and peril thus he wrought.
> When power his hands foresook,
>   Men with his teeth he firmly caught,
> And drew to safety up
>   Beside him on the rocky steep.
> Thus sixty lives or more,
>   He rescued from the hungry deep.

In all, some 200 passengers and members of the crew passed over the lines to the rock, but many of those who had taken to the rigging were unable even to start the journey by making the perilous crossing from where they clung to the point on the ship's rails to which the lines were lashed. Help must surely come soon, they believed, and to leave what seemed to be the safety of the rigging to stumble down the steeply sloping deck, with every chance of being washed off, and then entrust themselves to a strand of rope across yards of heaving water, was more than they could do. They had, too, the comforting presence of Mr. Firth who had taken up his stand in the mizzen rigging after his attempts to clear away the lifeboats had failed. Firth made no secret of the fact that he could not swim, and that come what may he intended to stay where he was. In the creeping light of dawn the survivors could see, too, from their vantage point, the number who failed to get across.

The ship's superstructure was beginning to break up under the pounding of the waves and William Hogan saw Quartermaster Williams sail off the ship on a makeshift raft made from the roof of the wheelhouse. The raft floated near the rock and when the quartermaster waved Hogan thought he was safe, but a wave caught the flimsy structure and dashed it against the granite and another following hurled it bodily some 6 ft up upon the stone. Williams fell off and when the water receded, taking the raft with it, he fell into the sea. Hogan thought he must have been severely injured for although he could see him struggling in the water he made no attempt to clamber back up the rock and eventually he disappeared under a welter of foam.

Hogan and Leahy were surrounded by some 15 or 20 German passengers, many of whom were crying piteously while others prayed. Hogan had considered making a try for the rock along one of the life-lines, but the rock looked as though it was covered with ice and there were dark objects on it which he thought might be sea-lions. Hogan asked someone to fetch a hatchet so that he could defend himself if they attacked him. No hatchet could be found and so Hogan stayed where he was, and it was only as it became light that he realised that the "sea-lions" were the bodies of his dead companions.

As the light became stronger Leahy noticed that more and more of those who tried to cross over were too cold and numb to hold on after their night in the rigging, and either let go half way over or else were too weak to climb up the rock on the other side. Those in the rigging were little better off, and it was only by constantly moving up and down that Leahy prevented himself from freezing. Many were already frost-bitten and on all sides men were dropping from exhaustion or were being washed off by the crashing waves which never ceased to pour over the hulk. Cyrus Fisher and his wife reached the deck and were trying to go forward to the lines when such a wave curled over the ship. A friend who saw it coming and held fast to a door reached out his hand to Mrs. Fisher but with a cry of "Save my husband!" she fell beneath its onslaught and as the water poured back into the sea Mr. Fisher went with it in a despairing, futile, attempt to save his wife.

From his place in the rigging, Charles W. Allen, a saloon passenger, could see what looked to be a well-found lifeboat that might have been launched, had there been any seamen there to do it. Spencer Jones took his chance on the lifeline and got safely across, but Nicholas Brandt, his companion, elected to stay in the rigging, thankful enough to be where he was now that daylight revealed the full plight of those on the rock, for the tide was rising and many of the survivors were too weak to keep their footing on the wet and slippery surface.

Help was not now far away, however. After stumbling about the island for half the night, Thomas found a deserted signal station and by shouting until he was hoarse finally aroused the attention of Thomas Clancey, a fisherman. Clancey took him to his house but Thomas refused to stay there. Telling the man to rouse the people and tell them a liner was ashore off the island, he borrowed a length of rope and retraced his steps to the beach.

Conditions on the rock were rapidly becoming impossible as the rising tide narrowed the area of usable surface. Brady implored Speakman to swim again with the halyard, this time from the rock to the island. Speakman said he was completely exhausted and that the sea was running too high but Brady told him "For God's sake, go! See what souls you will save!"

Speakman said the sea would dash out his brains against the rocks if he attempted it and while they debated the point they saw a group of men on the island carry the body of Quartermaster Purdie from the shore.

One of the men was Thomas and with the knowledge that help now lay on the other side Speakman elected to try to get across. Signalling to Thomas that he was coming over he tied the line round his waist and again plunged into the water. Thomas waited until the struggling swimmer was within his maximum reach and then with all the skill of a trained seaman he hurled the fisherman's line over the foaming water and right into Speakman's outstretched hands. Strong arms quickly pulled the exhausted man ashore, and now they had a line of communication from the ship to the rock and from the rock to the island, but many of the survivors were far too tired to make another crossing like that and of the 200 or so who landed on the rock, only about 50 were able to reach Mosher Island. For many, like Hugh Christie, the chief steward, the second crossing cost them the last ounce of their strength and they were forced to leave go of the rope, with safety in sight and despite the hands which reached out to save them.

Shipwreck!

Brady got across, however, and after a quick consultation with Thomas and a word with the fishermen he held up a board for Captain Williams to see. Written on it were the words: "BOATS ARE COMING".

The first boat was too small, being little more than a skiff. Speakman had found it when he went to Clancey's house to get warm and with the aid of some other survivors he carried it back to the beach and launched off in it. Hogan saw it coming and was bitterly disappointed to find that the seas were so heavy that the little boat could not get near enough to rescue the people on the ship or the rock. Fifteen minutes later Brady re-wrote the message on his board: "CHEER UP. THE BOATS ARE COMING".

It was another half hour, however, before the first large boat manned by Dennis Ryan, Frank Ryan, James Coolin, John Blackburn and Benjamin Blackburn set off and the crew's first action was to take three boatloads consisting of about 36 persons off the rock. While they were carrying out this operation Captain Williams shouted from the ship that they were in greater danger than the people on the rock, and that he would give $500 for every boatload taken from the ship. At this the boat started taking the people from the ship and took off another two boatloads before a second craft appeared, manned by James O'Brien, Michael O'Brien, Patrick Dollard, William Lacey and T. J. Tooig. These two boats were speedily joined by a third commanded by Brady.

Brady particularly wanted to take off Captain Williams and Fourth Officer Brown who all the while had been encouraging the passengers to use the lifelines and whom he knew must be exhausted. At first they refused to leave until he had filled his boat with passengers but at last they did foresake the ship and Captain Williams allowed himself to be helped ashore.

Hogan also came off in Brady's boat and when he left there were, he thought, about 80 people still remaining on the side of the ship and in the rigging. They were, however, quite cool and confident now of being rescued. Hogan, being wet through to the skin and exhausted from the cold, stumbled to Clancey's house where he was treated, along with the rest, with the greatest care.

In about an hour's time, after getting warm, he went back to the beach, to be greeted by a fearful sight. Some of those in the rigging were clearly stiff and dead while the others, the ones he had seen fall over the side, lay strewn on the beach in all directions. Finding nothing useful to do, Hogan and some others rowed across to the mainland at Lower Prospect and there joined Foxley, some other engineers and about 15 passengers who had decided not to impose upon the meagre accommodation in the village any longer but to walk to Halifax. Starting at half past one in the afternoon they made slow progress due to there being a foot of snow in places, but after stopping for refreshment at two houses and leaving behind three of their number who could walk no further, they at last arrived in the city just before 11 o'clock. Word of their coming had preceded them and they were directed speedily to Halifax Police Station where preparations had been made take care of them.

Brady had earlier sent a messenger on horseback into Halifax to report what had happened to the White Star Line's agents, S. Cunard & Co. Later in the afternoon, bruised, worn out but gradually getting warmer in an eating house in Upper Water Street, he gave the story to the world through the medium of a Halifax *Morning Chronicle* reporter who tracked him down.

"When I left the wreck at noon," he said, "all who were alive had been rescued except the chief officer, Mr. Firth. He was still in the rigging, holding on for life, and crying for assistance, but the sea had become so rough that no boat could venture out."

"Would he be saved?" asked the reporter.

"I fear not," Brady replied. "He must have been almost exhausted when I left and he could hardly hold out until the sea became calm enough for a boat to venture out. I tried to get some volunteers to go, but all said it would be certain death."

The death of the chief officer was included in the world headlines but Brady had not reckoned on the courage and skill of the Rev. William J. Ancient, the Church of England minister at Terence Bay.

At daylight Firth had counted 32 persons in the mizzenmast rigging, including a woman and a boy, 12-year-old John Hindley, of Ashton, Lancashire. Some were washed off while others made their way to the lifelines and either crossed to safety or died in the attempt, and by noon only Firth, the woman and the boy were left. John Hindley had been separated from his mother, father and brothers for many hours and did not know that they were dead, but the cheerfulness of the chief officer kept him in good spirits, though what little strength he possessed was fast fading away. Firth had secured a firm hold of the woman and had fastened her in the rigging but although she bore her ordeal with tremendous strength, in the end she, too, succumbed to the awful cold, her half-naked body and protruding eyes rendered more ghastly by the contrast with the jewels which still sparkled on her fingers. Now only Firth and the boy remained but although they could see those on the shore and could hail the men in the boats, they could not reach them.

At his house two miles away, where he served as a missionary for the Colonial Church Society, Mr. Ancient had been one of the first to hear about the wreck and had spent the morning caring for the survivors. Not until two o'clock in the afternoon was his attention directed to the man and the boy still in the rigging, and by that time the fishermen were hauling up their boats.

Mr. Ancient went to Mr. Edmund Ryan, the local magistrate who had taken charge of the rescue operation, and protested: "The water is smooth enough! You can get alongside in a boat!"

"You can get alongside," Mr. Ryan agreed, "but you cannot get at them when you get out there."

Thirty-six years old, 6 ft tall and strongly built, Mr. Ancient had been a scripture reader in the Royal Navy and during his six years at Prospect his genial appearance, bright eye, clear head and warm heart had won him a firm place in the affections of the people.

"Give me a boat and some men," he told Mr. Ryan. "Put me on board, and I will get them."

A volunteer crew was soon mustered comprising Patrick Duggan, Samual White and James Power, from Upper Prospect; John Blackburn, of Lower Prospect; and Joseph Slaughenwhite, of Terence Bay; but when they neared the wreck they refused to put the minister aboard, believing they were sending him to his death.

"If I am doomed, I won't hold you responsible," Mr. Ancient entreated them. "Put me aboard!"

Still they held off and while they backed and filled John Hindley fell from the rigging, but the fishermen's boat swept in and strong hands plucked the boy from the water, the only child of all the *Atlantic's* children to survive the wreck. Wrapping a coat around him they handed him into eager arms ashore and put out once again under Mr. Ancient's pleas to put him on board the ship. Finally they agreed, but it took all Mr. Ancient's massive strength to pull himself up the steeply sloping side of the ship. Once aboard he made his way to a lifeboat davit where he found a length of rope which he lashed securely to the rail. Taking the other end he made his way as close to Firth as he could get, and when he could go no further he stopped and shouted out;

Shipwreck!

"You are an officer, are you not?"

"Yes," Firth replied.

"Then you know how to make a bowline," said Mr. Ancient, and hurled the rope at him. "Now put your confidence in me and move when I tell you."

Firth followed his directions as the minister led him along by the rope, taking in the slack as he went. Whenever he slipped, which was often, the rope and the strong arms of the minister held him up until one wave, greater than the others, swept over them both and Firth was washed off.

"O Lord," Mr. Ancient heard him cry. "I have broken my shins!"

"Never mind your shins, man, it is your life we are after!" yelled Mr. Ancient as he hauled him back aboard again and into the main rigging, from which position it was a comparatively simple matter to lower him into the waiting boat.

There was nothing more to be done for those who had set out with such high hopes of a promised land across the Atlantic ocean. Mr. Ancient turned his boat towards the shore, bearing with him the last survivor of the worst disaster to a merchant ship the world had ever known.

Chapter Six

"Through Want of Proper Management"

NEWS of the disaster was first received in Halifax as some macabre All Fool's Day joke but when it was confirmed, three ships, the Dominion Government steamer *Lady Head*, carrying a number of Customs officers, the Cunard steamer *Delta*, with several newspaper reporters on board, and the tug *Goliah* were despatched at three o'clock in the morning of April 2nd so that they might reach the scene at daylight. Frowning and dangerous as the place was, there was a grandeur and beauty in the scene on that bright morning with the still angry waves beating against the rocks and enveloping the shore almost continually in clouds of glistening spray. Those on board the relieving steamers, however, had no time to waste in admiring the beauties of nature. Only the *Goliah* was small enough to venture among the islands on which the survivors were being cared for by the fishermen and their families but with the tug and a lifeboat acting as ferries the *Lady Head* and the *Delta* quickly filled with men from the *Atlantic*.

"And such a motley party!" wrote one of the reporters aboard the *Delta*. "Falstaff's ragged regiment were well attired and respectable looking compared to these. English, Irish, Scotch, Welsh, Germans, Dutch, Norwegians, Swedes, Swiss—indeed, representatives of every country in Europe and of the United State of America were huddled together talking, laughing, crying, praying and thanks-giving, producing a confusion of tongues of the most confused character. Scarcely one had a complete and respectable looking suit of clothes. The wealthy merchant of London and New York, the high toned professional gentleman and the lowest of the foreign emigrants appeared in strange clothing much of which had been given to them by the good people of Prospect.

"Some were without coats, many without hats, others without boots, and all had to mourn the absence of some comfort in the clothing line. Expensive broadcloth blended with the rough guernsey jacket on the one person. Here was an aristocratic looking man striving to make himself at home under a dilapidated looking overcoat that had probably done duty in days of yore on the back of more than one hardy fisherman of the place, while at the same time he made desperate efforts to get on his benumbed hands a pair of lavender kid gloves. He had a preference for kid as a rule, no doubt, but at that particular moment he was gazing enviously on a half-frightened-to-death Dutchman who sported a prodigious pair of wool mitts which did credit to the skill and sense of the fisherman's pretty daughter who had given them to him . . . .

"The *Delta's* passengers, in number 320, landed at the Cunard wharf late this afternoon (April 2). They were mostly men from 20 to 25 years of age. Many were in a pitiable condition—without shoes, feet swollen and bruised, clothes torn and drenched, some with bits of carpet, matting and blankets around them, and all fretted and sick from exposure all night. On reaching the locality it was found that a considerable number more than first named had been picked up and saved, among whom were some old and feeble persons who died after being rescued from exhaustion and cold."

With the fall of the tide the *Atlantic* broke in two abaft the foremast and before he left the scene, Captain Williams detached a party of seamen to keep watch, partly for bodies that might come ashore but also to prevent anyone carrying off items of cargo which were being washed out of the ship.

On his arrival in Halifax he gave the Customs authority to employ what labour they required for salvage, with the understanding that the salvage award should not be over 40 per cent of the net value, and if this was objected to, to leave it to the arbitration of two Justices of the Peace. There was another duty to be performed, and Captain Williams gave orders that a carpenter should prepare some 200 shells in which to bury the dead, and obtained the services of an undertaker to attend to the saloon passengers' bodies and that of the second officer, in case their relatives should want them forwarded.

The news of the disaster created a sensation everywhere, but nowhere more than in Liverpool. On the Exchange, in the Assize Courts and the Town Council and at the corner of every street, nothing else was talked about. First intimation was a telegram from J. H. Sparks, the White Star Line's agent in New York, stating that the ship had been wrecked off Halifax and that 700 lives had been lost. This announcement was posted in the Exchange Newsroom and was also published in the second edition of the *Liverpool Daily Post* for April 2.

For a time, people appeared overpowered by the magnitude and appalling character of the disaster—the largest loss of life at sea since H.M.S. *Association* and her consorts ran aground on the Scillies in 1707—but as the news spread, Water Street became thronged with people trying to get to the White Star Line's offices to find out the names of those lost—and those saved. This was something that even the owners could not tell them; the first Ismay himself knew of the disaster was when he saw a newspaper placard as he entered the city, but at half past nine another telegram arrived, confirming the news but giving no more detail.

In London, the Board of Trade learned of the loss through Sparks' first telegram being published in *The Times*, and immediately requested Ismay, Imrie & Co. to send "all particulars of the alleged loss." An account from Brady arrived by telegraph during the afternoon and the company were able to comply with the Board's request, but because Brady left the scene early his story contained a number of discrepancies, and even on matters which he reported accurately, he was disbelieved. His statement that the *Atlantic* had been putting in to Halifax for coal seemed so unlikely that Liverpool shipping circles discounted it and assumed the ship had suffered a technical defect which required immediate repair.

A telegram from Captain Williams received by Ismay, Imrie & Co. on the morning of April 3 put an end to this conjecture, and also showed that the loss of life had not been quite as bad as at first reported. "The ship totally lost," said Captain Williams. "Broken abaft the foremast. Cargo washing out. Wreckers at work until the New York Wrecking Company come. Thirteen saloon passengers and 429 others saved. Purser, chief steward, second officer and fifth engineer lost; the rest of the officers saved. Shall leave the third officer and four men at the wreck to attend to the bodies. Will forward passengers to New York and Portland and 200 go tomorrow, and the balance next day. The cause of our coming to Halifax was that we were short of coals. The wind is rising from the south and the wreck is exposed to the sea. The passengers are supplied with all necessities."

Although there had been a considerable reduction from the 700 death roll first reported, the fact that no women or children had been saved, coupled with confirmation of the fact that the *Atlantic* was putting in for bunkers, brought down a spate of criticism on the shoulders of Ismay, Imrie & Co. In the belief, too, that the ship had run aground through some defect of navigation, the Board of Trade ordered an official inquiry to be held, and Ismay, Imrie & Co. felt compelled to write to *The Times*.

"Although much and painfully depressed," they said, "by the grievous loss of life which has attended the shipwreck of the steamer *Atlantic*, and disinclined, therefore, to obtrude ourselves upon public attention, we feel that it is our duty, as managers of the Oceanic Steam Navigation Co., to which she belonged, to take notice of a statement in your columns to the effect that she was insufficiently supplied with coals.

"We submit that the facts are otherwise, for we are in a position to prove that the quantity put on board this vessel before leaving Liverpool was 967 tons, and that her consumption for the outward passage to New York upon an average, taken over the 18 voyages which she had successfully accomplished, was only 744 tons, while the largest quantity ever consumed on the worst winter passage, say in December and January, never exceeded 893 tons.

"We have three distinct and independent checks upon these figures, recorded in writing at the time of the vessel's departure, all of which agree within a few tons, 967 being the minimum which they establish as having been taken on board.

"We feel sure that you will consider that these figures are a complete answer to any charge of inadequate equipment; and we would add that it has throughout been our object and most anxious desire to provide all the vessels comprising this company's fleet with every possible requirement, without regard to cost.

"We have also endeavoured, and with much solicitude, to provide for their careful and safe navigation. We feel confident that a judicial inquiry into the loss of this fine ship, for which we are most desirous, will establish beyond doubt her excellent seagoing qualities and the completeness of her outfit in every department."

Having informed the Board of Trade that the decision to hold an inquiry met with their complete approval, Ismay, Imrie & Co. at once cabled Sparks in New York to send home the ship's officers as quickly as possible, so that they would be available to give evidence, but it was not to be. The Board of Trade were empowered under the Merchant Shipping Act to order an inquiry to be held into any casualty which occurred in British waters or which involved a British ship which was wrecked with loss of life in foreign waters, but similar legislation had also been enacted in Canada, and as the competent authority, the Department of Marine and Fisheries in Ottawa ordered an immediate inquiry to be held in Halifax. Ismay, Imrie & Co. were accordingly informed by the Board of Trade that the proposal to hold an inquiry in Britain had been countermanded.

The Halifax inquiry opened on Saturday, April 5, the court consisting of Edward M. Macdonald, Collector of Customs for the Port of Halifax, sitting as Wreck Commissioner, Captain George McKenzie, an experienced shipmaster, and Captain T. A. Scott, chairman of the Board of Examiners of Masters and Mates for Canada, as nautical assessors; and Charles J. Macdonald as clerk. The Hon. S. L. Shannon, Q.C., and H. Blanchard, Q.C., represented the Canadian Government and J. Norman Ritchie appeared for the master and officers.

The court thus presented a formidable array of nautical and legal talent and to open the proceedings Macdonald pointed out to Captain Williams that the inquiry would be equivalent to a Board of Trade inquiry in England. Any decision that might be arrived at, when approved by the Minister of Marine, would have the effect of a decision by a Board of Trade inquiry. He then asked Captain Williams and the other officers whether they were willing that the inquiry should proceed on that basis. After seeking advice from their counsel,

Captain Williams and the others agreed that the inquiry should start at once. It is doubtful, however, if they fully understood what was happening; Brown at least thought it was only a preliminary hearing and that the full Board of Trade inquiry would he held in Liverpool when they returned home. Even if that had happened, the outcome would probably have been the same.

Captain Williams admitted that he had probably misjudged the speed of the current and in his findings Mr. Edward Macdonald agreed with him. But he went on to say that the strength of the current only determined the precise spot where the *Atlantic* met the land; she would have struck somewhere anyway because of her excessive speed and lack of vigilance by her officers.

The night, said Mr. Macdonald, was one on which Sambro Light should have been seen some time before the disaster if a proper lookout had been kept. The fact that Captain Williams had left the deck at midnight, however, was calculated to create an impression in the minds of the officers on duty that they were not so near land as to make extra vigilance imperative.

But the greatest and the fatal error was failure to use the lead to find the depth of water under the ship.

"So accurate are the soundings laid down upon the chart," said Mr. Macdonald, "that had the lead been used at proper intervals the ship's safety would have been guaranteed, even had the night been one on which the lights could not possibly have been seen."

The neglect of this plainly manifest duty, he added, was so gravely at variance with what ought to have been the conduct of a man placed in a responsible position that he had been tempted to cancel Captain Williams' certificate of competency, a course which would have prevented him from sailing ever again as a navigating officer. Instead, because of what the Wreck Commissioner described as his judgement, coolness and bravery, and in consideration of the praiseworthy and energetic efforts which he made to save life after the ship struck, his certificate was suspended for two years.

Mr. Macdonald also had something to say about the fourth officer's conduct. Brown's action, he said, in preventing the steward calling Captain Williams at the appointed time was, under the circumstances, an improper violation of the master's orders. Also, as Brown was one of the officers-of-the-watch who might have seen the light but failed to do so, there was an implied culpable neglect of duty and want of vigilance. Brown's certificate, therefore, was suspended for three months as "a moderate punishment".

After the crew had left Halifax for England, Charles J. Macdonald (there were a lot of Macdonalds in Nova Scotia; this one was a notary public) certified a true copy of the findings for forwarding to the Hon. Peter Mitchell, the Minister of Marine and Fisheries, who had the power to confirm them or set them aside. Mitchell confirmed the findings, and submitted the minutes of the proceedings to the Privy Council of Canada. On the basis of these minutes and the findings of the court, a committee of the Privy Council drew up a further report which was then approved by the Governor-General. In this report, W. A. Heinsworth, clerk to the Privy Council, pointed out that the *Atlantic* had been lost "through the want of proper management on the part of the captain and officers of the vessel, and not on account of any defect in the lights on the coast of Nova Scotia".

He concluded: "The court is of the opinion that the vessel left port with an insufficient supply of coals on board. This is a serious reflection on the management of the shipping company, as it was the primary cause of the loss of the vessel."

During the period of the inquiry the steam tug *Henry Hoover* had been taking large parties out to view the wreck at a charge of $2 a head but soon the novelty wore off and it needed an impassioned plea in the Halifax *Morning Chronicle* to bring to the notice of the people of Halifax the plight of the fishermen of Prospect. The descent on them of over 400 cold, hungry and exhausted survivors had strained their resources to the limit. Their generosity had been unbounded, to such an extent that now they themselves were in need.

On the Sunday after the wreck the Rev. G. M. Grant, preaching in St. Matthew's, took the *Atlantic* as an illustration of the uncertainty of human life and the necessity of being always prepared for death. The *Morning Chronicle* was interested in more mundane things. "The fishermen's families gave all the provisions they had to the shipwrecked people, and in many instances are now themselves in actual want," it thundered. "There could be no better way to manifest sympathy in the matter than to send down to Prospect a quantity of provisions to refill the larders which were so cheerfully emptied to feed the distressed people."

Many responded to this plea and soon afterwards the Canadian Government, on the recommendation of the Minister of Marine, placed in the Supplementary Estimates the sum of $3,000 for the purpose of defraying expenses in connection with the burial of the dead and for conferring rewards. Of this sum, $1,560 was distributed among the people of Prospect and $700 was spent on providing coffins, but finding somewhere to bury them was another matter. The logical place would have been on a site close to the wreck but only a thin layer of soil covered the solid rock. There was only a small cemetery at Prospect and at the suggestion of the House of Assembly it was agreed that those recognized as Roman Catholic should be buried at Terence Bay and the others at Camp Hill Cemetery in Halifax itself.

Every shipwreck brings with it a crop of horror stories and the *Atlantic* was no exception. So strong were the accusations against the crew that they had robbed the dead that before he left Captain Williams personally examined as many bodies as he could as they were brought ashore. Many of them, he said, were bruised and disfigured from being knocked about among the rocks, but there were no signs of any such mutilations as had been reported. As an added precaution, however, he had every member of the crew searched as they came ashore from the *Delta*. Nothing was found on any of them to confirm the reports of robbery.

On the other hand, said Captain Williams, while the people of Prospect vied with each other in doing all they could for the living and the dead there were some who were intent only on plunder. They would seize bodies as they floated past, he alleged, or bring them up with a gaff, search the clothing for valuables and, unless they were in sight of other people, drop them back into the water again. Some bodies travelled a considerable way. That of a stewardess was picked up six miles away, and was found to have five sovereigns and ten shillings sewn into her clothing. One body was seen by the master of the *North American* floating in the water 20 miles south of Halifax. A William John Brindley had tried to save himself by putting on a cork life-jacket but while it kept him afloat it did not prevent him dying from exposure and his body was found at Lunenburg, 40 miles to the west of the wreck.

It is likely that those believed to have been plundering the dead were only seeking some relic of the disaster. Many were seen taking strange and curious articles from the shore—pieces of wood, large and small, from the ship herself or her furniture; bottles, cups and saucers and broken crockery; trees (there were some young fruit trees among the cargo); beads and shreds of cloth were all eagerly seized and borne away. The thing most generally sought after was a lock of hair from one of the dead bodies. Knives and scissors were freely used for a short time in obtaining tresses until those in charge of the salvage operations put a stop to these proceedings.

"Through Want of Proper Management"

The fishermen, however, may have looked upon the *Atlantic* as a gift falling right into their laps for there is no doubt that after their first and instinctive reaction to save life they carried out a beachcombing operation to some good effect. Only one action seems to have been brought, however. A fortnight after the wreck, James Slaughtenwhite, senior, of Terence Bay, was arrested on a charge of stealing property from the wreck. Mr. Shiels, the County Stipendiary Magistrate, was inclined to impose a severe penalty but at the request of the Customs, who said the object of the prosecution had been accomplished by the arrest of the man as a warning to others and that a term of imprisonment would seriously affect his fishing business, Mr. Shiels let him off with a fine of $10.

As well as the wish to reimburse the fishermen there was a widespread desire to reward the rescuers with something more than their out-of-pocket expenses and funds were opened in New York, Boston and Chicago, as well as throughout Canada, both for the rescuers and the rescued. Special financial provisions was made for little John Hindley but it was the Rev. Mr. Ancient—speedily and inevitably dubbed "The 'Ancient' Mariner" by the New York press—upon whom most of the praise was lavished.

"He should have a reception, a library and a medal," declared the *New York Star*. "Suppose we club together and give him something?"

Many did "club together", perhaps in response to one leader writer's cry that medals and pieces of plate were very nice but money was better, and in the end, Mr. Ancient did receive more money than medals. Despite a plea that the British Government should be recommended to give him the Albert Medal, the only award which Mr. Ancient seems to have received from across the Atlantic was the Silver Medal of the Liverpool Shipwreck and Humane Society. This society also gave £25 to Mr. Ancient to distribute among Mr. Clancey, his daughter, Mrs. S. A. Reilly, and others "for their great humanity and unwearied exertions in aiding the poor shipwrecked sufferers". From the Canadian Government, however, both Mr. Ancient and Edmund Ryan received gold watches worth $120 and Mr. Ancient received an additional $500 in cash. In later life, after he had received an honorary Master of Arts degree from King's College, Windsor, Nova Scotia, and been appointed diocesan secretary-treasurer, his most vivid memory of the *Atlantic* disaster remained Firth's solicitude for his shins. He died on July 20, 1908, at the age of 72.

Canadian sources also suggested that Chief Officer Firth, Third Officer Brady, the three quartermasters and the crews of the rescue boats should be recommended to the Royal Humane Society in London as being worthy recipients of their awards, but again it was only the Liverpool society which recognized their gallantry with an award of £2 each to Thomas, Speakman and Owen, and a later superior award to Thomas.

Thomas remains something of a mystery. That he was outspoken to the point of being insolent is certain and the officers probably disliked him because he appeared to have greater knowledge than they possessed themselves. Captain Williams disbelieved his statement that he warned the second officer that the ship had run her distance. "No officer," he said, "would have allowed such a breach of discipline." Brown confirmed that no quartermaster had made any such observation to the second officer in his hearing, but he did agree that Thomas suggested to him that he should go to the main yard and look for signs of land. After the disaster Thomas's part in the rescue operation was discredited by the surviving officers, who maintained that he did little or nothing after the ship struck.

Thomas retaliated by having an affidavit, signed by 26 members of the crew, sworn before Mayor James Duggan, of Halifax, a course of action which would have occurred to few of the mainly uneducated merchant seamen of the day. The affidavit said it was "mainly through the undaunted courage of Quartermaster Robert Thomas that we owe our lives." Clancy was also prevailed upon to swear "that Quartermaster Thomas was the first man ashore, and that he went to his house and gave the alarm, and that he worked bravely in saving life on the shore."

Thomas may have been protesting too much, but there is no doubt that he was a brave man. As a seaman aboard the *City of London* in 1865 he formed part of a lifeboat crew which rescued survivors from the *Ibis*, an action for which he was awarded the Silver Medal of the Liverpool Shipwreck and Humane Society. After giving him his £2 for his part in the *Atlantic* rescue the society received several letters from Halifax stating that Thomas had "returned to the scene of the disaster and at the risk of his life had conveyed a rope to a rock, by which means 50 or 60 persons were saved." This action should have been ascribed to Speakman but on the strength of the Halifax recommendation the Liverpool society awarded Thomas a clasp to his Silver Medal and £3. He had not long returned from Halifax when he received another clasp, this time for jumping from the *Lancashire* in the River Mersey to rescue a man who had fallen from Woodside landing stage while drunk. Some time after this he got a job with the Mersey Docks and Harbour Board and was serving in a lightship in April, 1875, when a man fell from a buoy tender and was in danger of being crushed between the tender and the buoy which it was attending.

Thomas again jumped overboard but fell heavily on to the angle iron edge of the buoy. He saved his man, and received another clasp, but he had suffered internal injuries in his fall and there are no further records of him performing any more rescues.

For many people, a simple letter of thanks was possibly more cherished than any medal would have been. A group of German passengers tendered their thanks all-embracingly to "the citizens of Halifax". John Foxley and five of his engineers singled out Mr. J. Doull and Mr. Nichols as the ones who had helped them most. Six members of the crew remembered particularly Mr. Silver, Mrs. Smith and Mrs. Robar. Many paid tribute to Captain Williams, but there were no medals for the master.

"To think," he said afterwards, "that while hundreds of men were saved, every woman should have perished—it's horrible. If I had been able to save even one woman I could bear the disaster better, but to lose all—it's terrible, terrible!"

Captain Williams knew that guilty or not, the world would hold him responsible, and the findings of the court of inquiry and the penalty they imposed came as no surprise. Some, however, were more vindictive than others. Charles W. Allen, one of the passengers, claimed that more could have been done to launch the *Atlantic's* lifeboats and went on record as one of those "saved" from the disaster. Saved he certainly had been, and he had no reason to emphasize the word in such a manner but the content of his complaint to the Board of Trade shows his frame of mind.

"Captain Williams," he wrote, "played cards for money daily in the smokeroom, and on some days in the saloon, and his so doing was the subject of conversation between myself and other passengers. In the interest of Atlantic passengers, I believe it would be a good thing that such practices should be forbidden."

James Brown, of Lindridge, near Teignmouth, was even more outspoken. Brown lived with his married daughter, Jane Kruger, and her three children, James Charles, Alfred Eugene and Herman Sinclair. Her husband, Herman Auguste Kruger, had sailed as a saloon passenger in the *Atlantic* and had lost his life on the rock strewn coast of Nova Scotia; a James Brown was among the saloon passengers saved but James Brown of Lindridge never gave any indication that he possessed first-hand knowledge of the disaster. But he did read the newspapers, and what he read displeased him greatly.

"The judicial inquiry at Halifax," he wrote, in a letter to T. H. Farrer, Permanent Secretary to the Board of Trade, "has terminated in so extraordinary a verdict that I, as one of the many suffering relatives of one of the victims, am construed to take the liberty of asking you whether this Halifax inquiry is to be final? For the credit of the Government of this country, I trust such will not be the case. The calamity in question was no accident; it did not result in any way from any unavoidable condition of the elements. The causes clearly enough stated in evidence were parsimony and culpable negligence in the management at Liverpool, subsequently followed by a reckless abandonment of duty on the part of the captain and other chief officers when nearing Halifax; indeed so utterly indifferent does the conduct of those men as to the safety of the ship before striking appear to have been, that if instructions had been given to them to run the vessel ashore, they could in no way have better succeeded in doing so.

"Such culpable dereliction of duty approximates more to murder than manslaughter, and so sweeping a sacrifice of upwards of 600 lives from causes so entirely within the control of those owning and navigating the ship, ought, for the credit of the Government of this great country, to be thoroughly investigated. I hope, therefore, to hear that a judicial inquiry of the most searching character either has been, or immediately will be, ordered to be held in England."

This letter eventually found its way to the desk of Thomas Gray, head of the Marine Department of the Board of Trade. Gray joined the Board as an 18-year-old clerk in 1851, the year after "An Act for Improving the Conditions of Masters, Mates and Seamen and Maintaining Discipline in the Merchant Service" had received the Royal Assent. This Mercantile Marine Act of 1850 gave the Board of Trade "general superintendence of matters relating to the British Mercantile Marine" and to carry out this work a Naval Department was formed which later became known as the Mercantile Marine Department. By 1862, Gray had become head of this Department's wreck and salvage branch and in 1866, following a reorganization of the Board into four main divisions, he was promoted to the Civil Service rank of assistant secretary and made head of the Marine Department.

Although he was tied to an office desk, Gray was passionately devoted to ships and the sea, and especially to the welfare and safety of seamen. He took the lead in shaping what has since developed into legislation affecting shipping which has become a pattern for all maritime nations, but in particular he studied the Collision Regulations, even to the extent of putting them into rhyme as an aid to learning by ships' officers. In the incident quoted earlier when the *City of Paris* crossed the *Atlantic's* bow, the officer-of-the-watch of the *Atlantic* was possibly muttering one of Gray's mnemonics:

> Both in safety and in doubt
> Always keep a good look-out;
> In danger, with no room to turn,
> Ease her, stop her, go astern!

For all his aptitude for rhymes of nursery quality, Gray was a martinet when it came to applying regulations and when he received the report of the Halifax inquiry he sent it to the Home Office, pointing out that a great number of lives had been lost, and drawing attention to the 239th section of the Merchant Shipping Act of 1854 which read: "Any member of, or any seaman, or apprentice belonging to any British ship who, by wilful breach of duty, or by neglect of duty, or by reason of drunkenness, does any act tending to the immediate loss, destruction or serious damage of such ship, or tending immediately to endanger the life or limb of any person . . . shall, for every such offence, be deemed guilty of a misdemeanour."

The Coal was there for Burning

In the absence of a public prosecutor, and because of pressure of work in the office of the Treasury Solicitor, the Home Office were frequently unable to undertake the prosecution of erring seamen, but the case of the *Atlantic* was outstanding both in the number of lives lost and the severity of the censure contained in the Wreck Commissioner's findings. After referring the facts to the law officers for their opinion, the Home Office informed Gray that a prosecution would at once be instituted against Captain Williams. No positive action was taken, however, pending a change of government, and in the event, the new law officers who were appointed thought the prosecution useless and it was abandoned.

Captain Williams thus escaped an action which could have led him to prison, but his situation still left much to be desired. Without his certificate he could not obtain a position at sea in any officer capacity, and as the sea was the only job he knew he applied to Gray for a certificate of lower grade than the one which had been suspended. "I have a wife and three children dependent on me," he said, "and I have no way of supporting them save in the exercise of my profession."

Gray would have none of it, however, and pointedly addressed his reply to Mr. J. A. Williams.

Captain Williams accepted the refusal but John Brown was more persistent. He had obtained his master's certificate shortly before joining the *Atlantic* and only learned that he had lost it for three months when he returned home and read a report of the court's findings in *The Liverpool Mercury*. Immediately he wrote to the Board of Trade pointing out that he was the sole support of his widowed mother and her two other children, and asking for a certificate of competency as mate. The newspaper report had simply stated that his certificate as master had been suspended; in that case, Brown reasoned, not illogically, his certificate as mate should still be valid. Before the Board of Trade could reply Brown was offered a job either as mate or master, depending on his grade of certificate. He quickly wrote again to the Board of Trade, this time setting out his version of what had happened.

"I had not orders to let the captain's steward call the captain," he said, "nor yet orders to call the captain at any stated time myself; the second officer, who was on the bridge, and was in charge of the deck, had the orders. I knew nothing of the steward coming till he came to me, with a cup of cocoa in his hand, and asked where the captain was, if on the bridge. I told him, no, he was in the chartroom asleep. He then asked should he call him. I said I thought not, but if he went on the bridge, the second officer would tell him properly whether to call him or not. The steward went, and came back and told me he had not to call him then; the second officer said he would call the captain himself at three o'clock; this was at 2.40 a.m.

"It was my duty to go down the steerage, fore and aft, twice each watch. At about 1 and 3 a.m. are the times for the middle watch, to see that all the lights are out, and that the steward on watch is awake. At 15 minutes to three I went to the fore part of the saloon deck to look for the light. I could see nothing but water, so I took my lamp and went down the steerage on my rounds. Just as I got out, the ship struck, at about 3.15 a.m. I then tried to save what lives I could. I remained on the wreck till about eight o'clock, when I swam ashore by the line, to help and encourage them with the boats, as the people were dying so fast of cold. All the time I was on the wreck I was helping and encouraging the passengers to go by the lines. I got three lines on shore after the first one, which one of the quartermasters swam with, with a lifebelt on.

"When I was examined in Halifax, I was under the impression, as I was told it was only a premature inquiry, that there would be a final held in England, and under such impression I left Halifax on the 8th of April for Liverpool, in the steamship *North American*, before the judgment was given out. Had I been present, I should have explained the circumstances better, when I think I should have gone unpunished.

"If you will, gentlemen, charitably consider my misfortune, and do what you can for me, I shall feel grateful."

Gray took nearly a month to reply, and when he did it was to inform Brown that his certificate as master was the only one he had, and with that suspended he now held no certificate of any grade.

Brown, who lived at 18 Washington Street, Liverpool, next sought out Captain Williams at his home in Church Street, Bootle, not very far away, and from him he obtained a certificate testifying to his good character. "This is to certify," wrote Captain Williams, "that Mr. John Brown, late fourth officer of the steamship *Atlantic*, lost at Marr's Head on the 1st of April, 1873, did not receive from me personally any orders about calling me at 3 a.m., these orders were given to the senior officer-of-the-watch, Mr. Metcalfe. The orders he received were from the third officer, Mr. Brady, to let me know if any change occurred in the weather. With reference to the stopping of my servant with chocolate at 2.40 a.m., all that Mr. Brown did was to refer him to the second officer as to calling me; in all that Mr. Brown did he acted under the orders of his immediate superior officers, and in no way can he be connected with the loss of the ship. After the wreck he conducted himself as a good officer and a brave seaman."

Captain Williams had done his best, and armed with this testimonial Brown again went to the Board of Trade and told them he wanted an answer as soon as possible as the ship in which he had been offered a berth was due to sail in a week's time. Gray sent him a printed slip by return of post, acknowledging receipt of his letter, and Brown also replied by return: "My owners must have an answer from me respecting the situation, in the course of a day or two; therefore a decided reply from you as early as possible, whether I am to have a mate's certificate or not, will much oblige."

Gray told him his case would be considered "in due course" and Brown immediately dashed off yet another letter. "I once more ask for a *decided answer*," he emphasized, "whether I am to have it or *not*, as my owners must now have an answer from me."

Gray still did not hurry to reply and Brown's ship sailed without him, but it would have made no difference. Three days after she had gone, Gray wrote to Brown to tell him he could not have a mate's certificate.

While Captain Williams faced professional ruin, and Brown lost an excellent chance to rehabilitate himself, still there were those who were prepared to defend their actions, and none more emphatically than the passengers who had been on board the *Atlantic*. In an attempt, perhaps, to mitigate the harshness of some of the things that had been said at the inquiry and in the newspapers, the cabin passengers got together and issued the following statement:

"We, the rescued passengers of the unfortunate ship *Atlantic*, desire to express our gratitude and respect for the noble conduct exhibited by Captain Williams and all his officers during the terrible scene which ensued at the wreck of the steamer on the coast of Nova Scotia."

Brady, another man of high courage who failed to win any medals, very nearly lost his life while supervising the salving of the *Atlantic's* cargo. He was standing on the side of the wreck and in the act of stepping into a boat which was waiting for him, when a heavy sea washed across the wreck and swept him into the sea. With no rope to hold on to this time, and despite his heavy clothing, Brady succeeded in swimming back to the boat.

It was Brady's leadership which had inspired Speakman to carry the lifeline and this quality came to the surface again less than 12 months after the wreck of the *Atlantic*. In February, 1874, Brady was a passenger in the American ship *Pennsylvania* when a gigantic wave swept her master, mate and second mate off the open bridge and into the sea. There was no possibility of rescuing them and the *Pennsylvania's* third officer refused to accept responsibility for the ship. Brady assumed command and brought her safely through the storm and into Philadelphia. For his services he was awarded $1,000 by the *Pennsylvania's* owners, but, deeming this insufficient, he sued them and obtained an award of $4,200, still little enough considering he had saved the lives of several hundred passengers and seamen as well as a ship worth $600,000 and cargo valued at $250,000.

William Hoy, the sailor-passenger who saved men with his teeth, had already decided to give up the sea before the disaster and was on his way to America to seek farm work. Not liking it there, he returned to Ireland, married a local girl and emigrated again, this time to Australia. There he settled successfully, reared a family of eight 6 ft sons and daughters, and died peacefully in 1918 at the age of 69.

The surviving passengers were sent on their way from Halifax as soon as possible, some in the Steamer *Chase* and the remainder in the *Falmouth* to Portland, Maine. From there they went to Boston, where some $1,000 which had been collected was distributed amongst them, and then on to New York, their original destination. The casualty lists which preceded them had raised false hopes in some hearts and the wife of John Charles Graf, a German passenger, went mad when she found that he was not among the survivors after all. Another to suffer in this way was a Mrs. Elderwald, of Philadelphia. Mrs. Elderwald was to have travelled in the *Atlantic* with her daughter but was detained at the last minute. Her daughter, being eager to rejoin her husband and children in America, sailed without her and was lost. Mrs. Elderwald sailed in the Cunard liner *Frisia*, fully expecting to meet her daughter in New York.

Two young men from Oswaldthwistle should also have sailed in the *Atlantic* but one decided to get married first and take his wife with him on a later sailing and at the last minute—the day before sailing—the other man's sister decided to go with him, so he gave up his place in order to make preparations for her passage. Five married men and one bachelor from Oswaldthwistle did go, however, and only two were saved, William Booth and John Smith. Smith was one of those who made compiling an accurate list of lost and saved difficult; his real name was Glover and he was escaping from an affiliation order.

The disaster gave rise to considerable argument amongst naval architects, particularly concerning the *Atlantic's* length in relation to her beam. "Driven at enormous speed," said one correspondent to *The Times*, "she would run right up the reef, each wave banging her upon it at a different point on her bottom, and so smashing in two or more of her six watertight compartments. It is said she struck five distinct times. A broader and shorter boat, harder to force through the water, would probably have only smashed in one or two compartments and would, by the aid of the other compartments have floated for some time."

It was Sir Williams Fairbairn, however, a prominent civil engineer and bridge-builder, who most incensed both Ismay, Imrie & Co. and Harland & Wolff with his comments about the strength of the ship. If she had been half her length, he said, she would never have gone to pieces; she was, he claimed, "extremely weak for her length."

Appalled by such statements and by the popular conception that the ship had snapped in two like a dry twig, Edward Harland went to Nova Scotia to see the condition of the wreck for himself, and the sort of ground on which she had struck. He found she had jammed her bows so firmly into a crevice in the rocks that her hull had become immovable, even under the immense pressure exerted by the sea. Something had had to give way under the strain, and the fracture had occurred at the point of greatest leverage, at the bows. She had, said Harland, "twisted her nose off", not broken in two. Apart from the holes torn in her plates by the rocks she was perfectly sound, with not a loose rivet or a bolt started. Her masts, what were left of them, were perfectly in line, but, Harland concluded regretfully, even if she had been lying as conveniently as Holyhead and not in some remote part of Nova Scotia, she could not have been salvaged.

Salvage of the cargo was a different proposition and large quantities were raised by Captain John Sheridan and a crew of divers from the New York Coast Wrecking Co. The work was both difficult and dangerous and was at times rendered impossible by the weather, but by blowing holes in the side of the ship the divers were able to enter the hull more easily. This made the ship settle even lower in the water, however, and at a meeting in the Halifax Hotel the friends of the lost cabin passengers passed a resolution complaining that the managers of the White Star Line were not taking sufficient measures to recover the bodies of the dead. Hearing of this, Captain Sheridan offered to devote special attention to recovering the bodies, if he received $50 for every cabin passenger and $20 for every steerage passenger, the difference being due to the fact that the cabin was much more dangerous for the divers to enter. White Star accepted Captain Sheridan's offer and thereafter many more bodies were recovered. Sir Edward Harland's opinion of the salvage of the ship herself, however, was confirmed by the experts who had been down to see her and in September, 1873, after as much cargo as possible had been got out of her, the wreck was sold at auction for $4,000.

Chapter Seven

The Coal was There for Burning

AS far as Captain Williams and Fourth Officer Brown were concerned, the reaction in Liverpool to the Halifax court's findings was that they had got what they deserved, but shipping circles particularly were not prepared to accept so easily the court's remarks with regard to the White Star Line. There was undisguised disbelief that any Dominion court, conducted by a Collector of Customs and without the benefit of expert testimony, could arrive at a true decision on a problem so complicated as the coaling of a trans-Atlantic liner, and especially one belonging to a company with the reputation for efficiency possessed by the White Star Line. There were far too many unanswered questions.

"What quantity of coal was put on board?" asked the *Liverpool Daily Post.* "Who checked the quantity? What was the price? Did the quality correspond? Was that quality such as to render the quantity of coal put on board sufficient? And, supposing all these things to be proved, then, was the coal so stowed that it could be freely got at? And was it used with economy or with reckless extravagance? There ought to be no difficulty in answering these questions immediately, and till they are answered the White Star Company must lie under the full burden of the verdict of the Halifax inquiry."

The White Star Line, confident that a searching inquiry could only prove that the ship had been fully supplied with coal of the best quality, were the most eager of any that such an inquiry should be held, and quickly, before the reputation of the company suffered beyond repair.

Throughout Britain there was a considerable measure of wonder that a foreign, albeit Dominion, court should have the temerity to investigate the loss of a British ship, censure her officers, suspend their certificates and harshly criticise her owners. In short, asked Sir John Pakington, M.P., in the House of Commons, was the Halifax inquiry legal?

Chichester Fortescue, President of the Board of Trade, replied to the question.

"I am unable to give a complete answer," he said, "in consequence of the absence of the official minutes of the inquiry at Halifax, and until they have been received, I can only say what we know at present.

"The inquiry lately held at Halifax purported to have been held under the powers of a Colonial Act passed under the authority of the Imperial Merchant Shipping Act, under which the Dominion authorities have the power to hold inquiries in all respects similar to inquiries held in this country under the direct authority of the Merchant Shipping Act. Whether all proceedings in connection with the inquiry in Halifax were regular or not I am not able positively to say; I must, at the same time, say, according to our experience, that Canadian inquiries of this kind are generally well looked after.

"The result of the inquiry has been that the captain's certificate has been suspended for two years. If that inquiry has not been regular, it can be had over again in this country. If it

THE "ATLANTIC" DISASTER.

CAPT. WILLIAMS.
FROM A PHOTOGRAPH BY ROCKWOOD.

JOHN HINDLEY.
FROM A PHOTOGRAPH BY CHASE.

THE REV. MR. ANCIENT.
FROM A PHOTOGRAPH BY CHASE.

Credit: Public Archives of Canada.

Thomas Henry Ismay, founder of the White Star Line.

Credit: Cunard.

The S.S. *Atlantic*.   Credit: Cunard.

Artist's impression of the *Atlantic*   Credit: Public Archives of Canada.

THE S. S. "ATLANTIC," RECENTLY WRECKED NEAR PROSPECT, N. S.

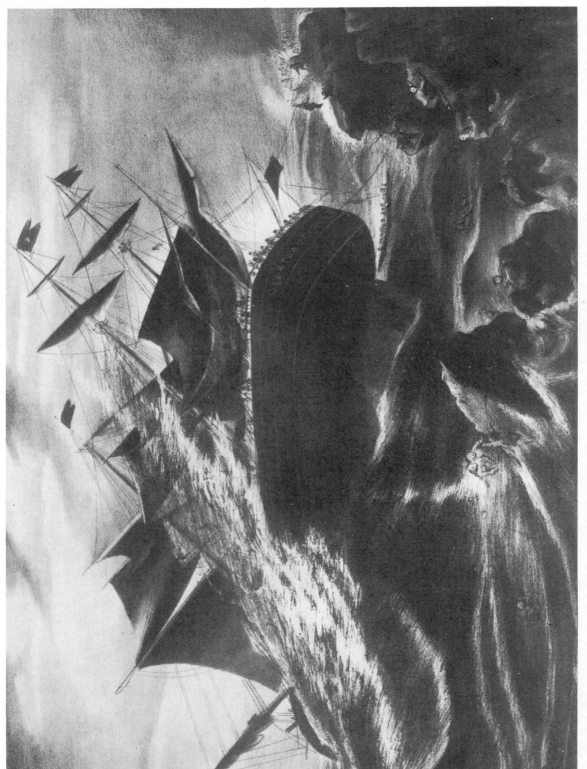

Artist's impression of the wreck. The ship did not in fact have her sails set when she stranded.

Credit: National Maritime Museum.

THE "ATLANTIC" DISASTER.—THE WRECK ON MEAGHER'S ISLAND.

Artist's impression of the wreck, with rescue craft.   Credit: Public Archives of Canada.

Sketch said to show the actual position of the wreck. Note the scattering of snow on the land in the background.
                                                                        Credit: Public Archives of Canada.

THE "ATLANTIC" DISASTER.—ACTUAL POSITION OF THE HULL.—FROM A SKETCH BY E. J. RUSSELL.

AN INCIDENT AT THE WRECK OF THE S.S. "ATLANTIC."

Artist's impression of "an incident at the wreck." This is intended to show the Rev. Mr. Ancient rescuing the chief officer.

Credit: Public Archives of Canada.

The wreck, barely showing above the water, holds little attraction for local people.   Credit: Harland & Wolff.

Salvage vessels at work.   Credit: Halifax Maritime Museum.

Waves breaking over the wreck.   Credit: Harland & Wolff.

Salvage vessels at work.   Credit: Halifax Maritime Museum.

has been regular, and in strict accordance with the law as far as concerns the captain, he cannot be tried over again. Whether any further investigations or other proceedings should be held affecting the captain or officers, it will be impossible for us to say until the official minutes shall have been received.

"There is another separate subject which must be inquired into in this country, namely, the allegations that the quantity of fuel and provisions on board the *Atlantic* was insufficient, and that this circumstance necessitated her going out of her course. This affected in the first place the conduct of her owners, and also the conduct of the officers of the Board of Trade, and into this matter, which can only be properly investigated at Liverpool, I have ordered a full and searching inquiry to be held. A wish that such an inquiry should be instituted was strongly expressed by the owners of the *Atlantic*."

Shortly afterwards, on May 6, 1873, Thomas Gray at the Board of Trade signed Memorandum M.6874 appointing Rear Admiral Charles Frederick Schomberg "to inquire and report whether the provisions of the Merchant Shipping Acts and of the Passengers Acts have been complied with in the case of the survey and inspection of the steamship Atlantic and of her rigging and equipments, and of the stores, fuel, and provisions put on board of her."

No time was lost in putting the machinery in motion. William Waldron Ravenhill, Recorder of Andover, was appointed legal assessor, the Local Marine Board in Liverpool were requested to furnish a room in which the inquiry could be held, and Ismay, Imrie & Co. were told of the steps which had been taken.

Admiral Schomberg belonged to a famous naval family. The eldest son of Vice-Admiral Alexander Wilmot Schomberg by his second marriage to a daughter of Rear-Admiral Richard Smith, he entered the Royal Navy from the Royal Naval College in May, 1827. Thirteen years later, while serving in the 72-gun ship *Hastings*, he took part in his one and only naval action. The British Mediterranean Fleet were operating against the Turks in Syria and Egypt and the *Hastings* was one of the ships engaged in the blockade and siege of Beyrout. Schomberg was among a party which went ashore in boats on a successful sabotage mission.

From the *Hastings* he went to the paddle steamers *Cyclops* and *Tartarus*, and after being promoted to Commander he became, in succession, second captain of the 110-gun ships *Queen* and *San Josef*, stationed at Devonport. After this period virtually spent ashore he was appointed to the 72-gun *Wellesley* on the North American and West Indies station. When he returned home in 1851 he was appointed captain and served as an emigration officer, first at Dublin and then at Liverpool. He then went in command of the 90-gun ship *Aboukir* with the Channel Squadron, but this sea appointment did not last long and was followed by a succession of shore posts, to the guardship *Cumberland* at Sheerness, the *Edinburgh* and the *Trafalgar* at Queensferry, and finally to command of the Leith district of the Royal Naval Coast Volunteers. Placed on the Retired List in 1864, he was appointed a rear-admiral in 1867 and given the post of Queen's Harbourmaster at Holyhead. Schomberg became a Vice-Admiral at the beginning of 1873, and despite his lack of knowledge of Merchant Navy matters in general, and coal-burning ships in particular, he had no hesitation in accepting the appointment as inspector for the Board of Trade. The Local Marine Board informed Gray that the inquiry could start on May 10 in the boardroom of the Liverpool Sailors' Home and G. Hamilton Fletcher, on behalf of the White Star Line, expressed the opinion that the company had been placed in such an unfavourable position that their evidence would have to be given "in that full and complete form which it is believed can only be fully attained under the guidance of counsel."

The Coal was there for Burning

In the light of subsequent events this was a wise decision. Throughout the inquiry, Schomberg ignored the fact that it was his duty to find out whether *or not* the *Atlantic* had been short of coal. Instead, he accepted the finding of the Halifax inquiry as being correct, and sought only to discover not if, but why, the *Atlantic* had been short. He soon arrived at a number of theories, and as witness succeeded witness, each theory was put to the test. The owners might have ordered a smaller quantity of coal than usual in order to save money. The coal ordered might have been sufficient but it might not all have been delivered. If it had all been delivered to the dock, then some might have been put aboard the wrong ship, or even stolen from the lighters. If it had all gone to the *Atlantic*, then it might have been used extravagantly, or it might have been of such poor quality that it had to be used generously in order to keep up a good head of steam. Although Ravenhill seemed to suspect it, not for a moment did it enter Schomberg's mind that Foxley's calculations, on which the Halifax findings were based, might have been wrong.

Giving evidence on the fourth day of the inquiry, Stewart Gordon Horsburgh, the White Star Line's superintendent engineer, said it was his firm belief that the coals were underestimated on March 31st; that there was in fact a larger quantity in the bunkers than was supposed.

Schomberg ignored this simple explanation and instead, having established that there had probably been sufficient coal on board to begin with, began to probe the possibility that it might have been consumed more rapidly than usual. In this, the court fell into the trap of thinking that a ship battling against a head wind would burn more coal than one sailing in calm water. In fact, a ship in such a situation, practically hove to and with her propeller turning just enough to keep her head to the wind, burns less coal. Horsburgh, who had served at sea as a chief engineer for 11 years, could not understand why the court failed to comprehend something which, to him, was obvious. But neither he nor any one else could convince Schomberg that the fault lay in Foxley's logbook and in his report to the Board of Trade the vice-admiral stated "We cannot but think that it would have been more judicious to have had a larger amount, say, at least 100 tons more fully on board her."

This report was not published but was sent privately to the White Star Line for their comments. To say it would have been more judicious to have another 100 tons on board was the same as saying that it was injudicious to despatch the ship with the amount she did have, and that was a reproach which could have led to serious consequences for the company. They therefore wrote to the Board of Trade setting out in exact terms their belief that the findings were not in accordance with the evidence.

"We trust that we may be permitted," said White Star, "to produce further evidence to show conclusively that 960 tons were (as in fact they were) a considerably larger quantity of coal than was necessary for us to have put on board the vessel for the voyage, and that we are by no means open to the serious and most prejudicial charge which the clause in question conveys."

Thomas Gray did not like Schomberg's indecisive report either. The Halifax findings represented a serious charge against the Board's surveyors, in that it was they who had permitted the ship to sail in the first place. If they hadn't done their job properly then Gray wanted to know; if they had, he wanted them exonerated. In addition, the White Star Line was rapidly gaining ascendency on the North Atlantic. It would do incalculable harm to Britain's prestige if the company collapsed, as it might well do if the travelling public gained the impression that its ships were unsafe. Gray wanted it settled one way or the other. He was not going to have the White Star Line and his surveyors vilified if they were innocent, but equally, he was not going to see them let off with a gentle reproach if they had been guilty of reckless disregard for the safety of life at sea which he held so dear.

The Coal was There for Burning

To Ismay, Imrie & Co., therefore, went a letter telling them that as it was of great importance to come to a sound conclusion, their further evidence would be heard. And to Schomberg went a letter telling him that the Board "thought it wise, under the circumstances, to request you to re-open the inquiry, so far as the question of fuel is concerned, by receiving and considering any further evidence which may be tendered on that point.

The first witness at the resumed inquiry was Sir Edward Harland and he immediately made the same point as Horsburgh had earlier; that the quantity of coal estimated to be on board was invariably less than the quantity actually present, and that engineers always entered in their logbooks a lesser quantity than there really was in the bunkers.

Both Schomberg and Ravenhill had great difficulty in understanding that storekeepers, whether they be marine engineers or not, like to keep a little in hand which doesn't show in the record.

"You told us," said Ravenhill, "that it is the custom for engineers to have a greater reserve of coal at the end of a voyage than they report; is that what I understand you to say? Will you be good enough to say why? What is the reason for that?"

"For this reason," said Harland patiently. "An engineer looks upon the coal as his supply of power, and if it turns out less than he expects then he cannot drive his engines. In plain terms, he likes to sing out before he is hurt."

The Liverpool shipping industry was a close-knit fraternity, rivals in business but linked by problems and conditions which were common to all. A slur cast upon one company could have reacted against all their interests, and Ismay's friends had not hesitated, when asked, to give evidence on his behalf. Sir Edward Harland was followed by Alfred Holt, founder of the Blue Funnel Line, Bryce Allan, of the Allan Line, and Alexander McLennan, superintendent engineer of the National Steamship Company. All swore that with 960 tons of coal on board the *Atlantic* had ample fuel to take her to New York. They would have sent their ships out on a similar voyage with just such an amount.

But the fact remained that the *Atlantic* had altered course for the very reason that there was insufficient fuel—or because her officers believed there to be insufficient. Called to explain his action, Captain Williams said he knew from Foxley's daily reports that the coal was getting low despite attempts to reduce consumption. On the morning of March 31st he had told Foxley not to stand upon his own judgment but to send all the engineer officers into the bunkers, each to make his own assessment of the coal remaining. After this Foxley had brought him a note to the chartroom saying there were 129 tons left.

At this point Ravenhill asked Foxley to leave the boardroom and wait outside. Captain Williams went on to explain how he had discussed the situation with his chief officer and the engineer and between them they had decided that the only prudent course open to them was to put into Halifax. At no time had Foxley suggested any other figure than 129 tons.

Firth supported this story but Foxley had a different tale to tell. He agreed that he had given Captain Williams a note with "129 tons" written on it but he swore that at the same time he had said there was enough coal for two days' steaming.

"We should remind you", said Ravenhill, "that the captain says it is not so. Therefore you are pledging your character and your oath against that of another man. Just recollect that. It is a very solemn thing you are doing now."

"I am giving my own observations," said Foxley. There were, he explained, something like 153 tons of coal left in the bunkers—20 tons in one, 45 in another, 80 in another and about eight in another. It was, he thought, about the same sort of amount as had remained on March 17th, before the coal had been loaded in Liverpool.

"How on earth, then," said Schomberg, "did you write down for the captain that there was only 129 tons?"

He had done it, said Foxley, to make the figure correspond with the reports he had given earlier. But, he insisted, he had also said there was coal enough for two days' steaming and nothing would shift him from it.

At the end of the second stage of the hearing Ismay submitted a number of engine-room logbooks for the court's consideration and armed with these and the depositions of the 46 witnesses who had been heard over the 14 days of the inquiry, Schomberg made a formal apology for having given everyone so much trouble and announced that the inquiry would be, not closed, but adjourned *sine die*.

A week later G. Hamilton Fletcher wrote to Thomas Gray to ask whether the White Star Line might be permitted to have a copy of the findings so that they could comment on them, if comment were deemed necessary, before they were presented to Parliament. White Star had had the foresight to employ their own shorthand writer, H. S. Mallet, a reporter with the *Liverpool Daily Post,* to take a verbatim note of the entire proceedings, and in a second letter to Gray on the same day, Fletcher suggested that he might like to have a transcript of Mallet's notes, for his more complete information.

Gray accepted the offer and Fletcher at once gave instructions not only for a complete transcript to be made of the 12,000 questions and answers that had passed but also set about making the company's own analysis of the evidence.

Before this task could be completed, although Mallet was said to be "pushing forward his work with all speed", Schomberg's findings, duly approved by Ravenhill, arrived at the Board of Trade. They were, Gray found, even harsher than the interim report, which had merely accused White Star of being injudicious. Now, Schomberg said, even the exact quantity of coal on board at the start of the voyage was uncertain because there had been no check on the weight after it left the collieries, none on the expenditure in port, and a conflict of opinions as to the amount of surplus from the previous voyage. He accepted that the daily consumption was 70 tons and fully believed Foxley's note which said there were 129 tons remaining because this was verified by the master and the chief officer. Foxley's assertion that he had said anything about "two days' steaming" was rejected.

His final report declared: "The decision that we came to on the provisional closing of our inquiry, viz. 'that it would have been more judicious to have had at least 100 tons more fuel on board', has been strengthened by further evidence to the conviction that the *Atlantic*, though in other respects well found and well equipped, was not supplied with sufficient coal of a quality suitable for a passenger ship of her class for a voyage to New York on the 20th of March last. We therefore share the opinion so admirably expressed in the judgment of the court in Nova Scotia, that Captain Williams was justified in bearing up for Halifax to obtain fuel.

"In arriving at the conclusion that the *Atlantic* was insufficiently coaled for this voyage, considering the character of the coal, we are compelled to differ with several gentlemen of well-known position and experience; but whatever probabilities there might have been of the coals said to have been on board proving sufficient, it appears to us that not enough margin was allowed for waste, bad stoking and the swift-burning character of the coal.

"No passenger ship of her class should be short of coal on the 11th day of her voyage to New York, as the *Atlantic*, in our opinion, undoubtedly was."

Within two days of receiving the findings, Fletcher had compiled a letter to the Board of Trade in which he protested against the adoption of a report "so contrary to the evidence on which it professes to be founded". He suggested that the truth might be arrived at better if the Board of Trade submitted the shorthand writer's transcript "to some gentleman who has a practical acquaintance with the requirements of a modern steamship".

The Coal was There for Burning

Thomas Gray agreed, and gave the transcript, White Star's analysis of the evidence, the logbooks and other documents involved in the case to two men who could be depended upon to know what was involved, J. MacFarlane Gray, the Board of Trade's chief examiner of engineers, and Thomas W. Traill, the Board's chief engineer surveyor.

Their report, issued as a Government Blue Paper early in 1874, completely vindicated White Star. "It is, no doubt," they said, "owing altogether to the purely engineering character of the questions that the naval officer and barrister who have heard the evidence have thought statements to be conflicting, which would appear to an engineer to be in perfect agreement. They are all purely engineering questions, and we are therefore not surprised that the Liverpool court, who are not engineers, should have been perplexed, and should have failed to discover the thread of consistency which is so apparent to us throughout the whole of the evidence."

Coal, they pointed out, could be measured to a fraction of an inch or weighed to a fraction of a grain, in a laboratory experiment. In practice it could not be weighed by the ton to within a few pounds and a supply of 1,000 tons might be right to within 10 or 20 tons, more or less. The estimates in such a case were, in practice, never supposed to be within anything but a very wide margin of the exact amount, and a wide, if reasonable, difference of estimates would never be treated by engineers as a "conflict of evidence". The witnesses had never supposed themselves either qualified or required to say what was the "exact" amount, and the Liverpool court had been asking for what could not possibly be told them, either for the *Atlantic* or for any other passenger steamer that ever existed, for in no single instance had coal quantities remaining ever been taken to the "exact amount" when over 100 tons remained, as there was in the *Atlantic*.

As far as the coals never having been weighed or measured, Traill and MacFarlane Gray were scathing at Schomberg's lack of commercial knowledge. Money was involved, they pointed out. The coals passed through the hands of five independent companies—colliery, railway, coal merchant, barge owner and shipping company—each of whom was paid by weight. There could be no doubt in the mind of anyone acquainted with such matters that if White Star paid for 847 tons then that was the quantity, near enough, which they received and that was the quantity put aboard the ship.

Traill and Gray did not believe that any of Foxley's figures were correct in terms of absolute measurement but they accepted them as reasonable logbook estimates. From their knowledge and long experience of trans-Atlantic coal-burning steamers they considered that irrespective of what Foxley put in his log as the daily consumption, the actual consumption of the *Atlantic* would not have exceeded 65 tons a day. Had it really been 70 tons a day it would have led Foxley to husband his resources much earlier in the voyage. To explain this they constructed the table (overleaf) starting at noon on March 21 when the *Atlantic* was 20 miles out from Queenstown with 2,811 miles to run to New York. The coal remaining, by the log account, was 979 tons less 150, a total of 829 tons.

If this statement had been true, said the experts, then the master and the chief engineer should have known from the beginning of the voyage that the ship was short of coal because the first day's consumption was one-eleventh of the fuel on board. The inference was that either Captain Williams thought it quite proper to start from Queenstown with only 11 days' consumption on board, or he never thought about the coal at all until he was told there was only 319 tons left.

But the statement was not true, they said, and had only been made out to tally with Foxley's account. "The following table" (overleaf) they explained, "is not constructed on any specific statements in evidence, but upon our conclusions, the grounds for which are fully

55

The Coal was there for Burning

	Daily Report				Stock of Fuel		
	Distance Accomplished and Coals Consumed				Remaining Coals and Distance to Run		
1	2	3	4		5	6	7
Dates	Miles Run	Miles per Ton	Coals Consumed		Tons Remaining	Miles to Run	Miles per Ton
21 March					829	2,811	3·39
22 March	324	4·32	75		754	2,487	3·30
23 March	300	3·99	75		679	2,187	3·22
24 March	294	3·92	75		604	1,893	3·13
25 March	196	2·61	75		529	1,697	3·21
26 March	118	1·69	70		459	1,579	3·44
27 March	244	3·49	70		389	1,335	3·43
28 March	189	2·70	70		319	1,146	3·59
29 March	238	3·40	70		249	908	3·65
30 March	264	4·60	60		189	644	3·41
31 March	169	2·81	60		129	475	3·68

[Coal consumption based on Foxley's figures.]

established in the evidence. When about 20 miles from Queenstown, at noon on the 21st, the coals on board would amount to 140 + 847 − 49 − 65 = 873 tons.*

They drew a line under March 31 as there their investigation should have ended, but as the question before them was: "Was the *Atlantic* short of fuel?" they continued the entries as they would have been had the ship continued to New York. They did not suppose any improvement in speed after the gale of the 31st and reckoned on only seven knots from her position on the 31st. Even under these unfavourable conditions, the table showed that the *Atlantic* would have got there safely.

"There is no doubt," Traill and Gray concluded, "that Captain Williams did what he thought was best when he decided to bear up for Halifax, and upon the statement made to him he was justified in doing so.

"In concluding our report we state that we are satisfied that the steamship *Atlantic* on her last voyage was supplied with sufficient coal for a voyage to New York at that season of the year, and that at the time the vessel's course was altered for Halifax there still remained sufficient coal on board to have taken her to New York and to leave 70 tons in the bunkers, even if the weather did not improve."

Just what was said in the chartroom before the change of course was ordered will never be known, but certainly Foxley was at fault in allowing Captain Williams to accept the book figure and for failing to emphasize that in fact there was more coal in the ship than showed in the log, enough in fact for "two days' steaming". But Foxley should not be blamed too much.

* Foxley estimated the coal remaining from the previous voyage as 132 tons in his log and 120 tons in his report; the coal stevedore's foreman estimated 140 tons and White Star's superintendent estimated 160 tons. The assessors accepted an average of 140 tons and added it to the 847 tons of new stock. They then estimated the consumption of the donkey boiler working for three days as four tons per day (12 tons) and a similar amount for the main boilers (12 tons); by knowing the capacity of the furnaces they estimated seven tons for coaling the bars and a further five tons for keeping the fires banked. They added 13 tons for getting up steam, undocking and lying for about eight hours with fires banked, making 12 + 12 + 7 + 5 + 13 = 49 tons. The 65 tons is for fuel consumed from 3 p.m. on the 20th until noon on the 21st and includes lying under steam from noon before starting and the fact that the engines were standing for an hour and a half at Queenstown.

The Coal was There for Burning

	Daily Report				Stock of Fuel		
	Distance Accomplished and Coals Consumed				Remaining Coals and Distance to Run		
1	2	3	4		5	6	7
Dates	Miles Run	Miles per Ton	Coal Consumed		Tons Remaining	Miles to Run	Miles per Ton
21 March					873	2,811	3·22
22 March	324	4·63	70		803	2,487	3·10
23 March	300	4·29	70		733	2,187	2·98
24 March	294	4·20	70		663	1,893	2·85
25 March	196	2·80	70		593	1,697	2·86
26 March	118	1·82	65		528	1,579	2·99
27 March	244	3·75	65		463	1,335	2·88
28 March	189	2·91	65		398	1,146	2·88
29 March	238	3·67	65		333	908	2·73
30 March	264	4·89	54		279	644	2·31
31 March	169	3·13	54		225	475	2·11
1 April	169	3·13	54		169	306	1·81
2 April	169	3·13	54		115	137	1·19
3 April	137	3·13	44		71	—	—

[Coal consumption according to Board of Trade assessors.]

Had the ship not stranded his error of judgement would not have made an atom of difference to anyone. Only through the negligence of others did it later take on the appearance of a colossal blunder, but there was no cause and effect. The loss of the *Atlantic* was not through her being driven on a lee shore, helpless, her fuel spent and her engines without power. She was run at full speed, engines and boilers all in perfect order, upon well-known rocks in reasonable weather. Indeed, so efficiently were her engines working that the vessel had actually over-run her distance at the time she struck. The choice of destination was Foxley's doing, but the manner in which the ship was navigated to that destination lay in other hands than his.

Exoneration for the White Star Line came too late to save them from much unjustified criticism but the company continued to prosper, although it was fated to be dogged by disaster at sea. The *Britannic* collided with the *Julia*, which sank, collided with the *Celtic* and sank the brig *Czarawitz*. The *Baltic* sank after striking a derelict and the *Belgic* broke her back on a sandbank in the River Mersey. The second *Oceanic* collided with the coaster *Kincora* and sank her and was later wrecked herself in the Shetland Islands. The *Gothic* caught fire, the *Noronic* disappeared without trace and the *Runic* achieved immortality when, after being sold out of the company and renamed *Imo*, she collided with a munition ship in Halifax harbour and blew up half the city. The *Republic* sank after colliding with the *Florida* and the *Cedric* collided with the *Montreal*. The *Olympic* rammed and sank the Nantucket lightship and in the most terrible peacetime shipping disaster of all time, the *Titanic* hit an iceberg on her maiden voyage and sank with the loss of 1,503 lives.

This was the toll that had to be paid to keep the White Star Line in the forefront of the trans-Atlantic companies. They were pioneers in vessel design, in size, in engine performance and output and in passenger amenities, and they chalked up an impressive record of fast Atlantic crossings. Like many of their contemporaries, they paid little in wages but gave generously to charity. The Merchant Navy, and particularly sick and elderly seafarers and

Chart showing position of the disaster.

Credit: Ministry of Defence (Navy).

their widows, still benefit from the bequests of the Ismay family. In 1887, the year of Queen Victoria's Golden Jubilee and his own 50th birthday, Thomas Ismay founded the Liverpool Seamen's Pension Fund with a gift of £20,000. In his will he left a further £10,000 to his wife to found the Margaret Ismay Widows' Fund. After the loss of the *Titanic* Thomas Ismay's son, J. Bruce Ismay, set up the Mercantile Marine (Widows) Fund with a gift of £10,000 from himself and £1,000 from his wife and after the First World War he established the National Mercantile Marine Fund with a gift of £25,000. These funds, which are today administered by the Mercantile Marine Service Association, now have total net assets of well over £1 mn.

Thomas Ismay died in November, 1899, and was succeeded as chairman of the company by his son, but three years later control of the company passed to the International Mercantile Marine Co., an American combine led by J. Pierpoint Morgan, although J. Bruce Ismay remained chairman and managing director of White Star and later became president of International Mercantile Marine. After the *Titanic* disaster he severed his active connection with both companies and retired to his home in County Galway.

In 1926 the White Star Line became British again when it was bought back from International Mercantile Marine by Lord Kylsant's Royal Mail Steam Packet Co. Under his control, the company placed an order with Harland & Wolff in 1928 for a liner of 60,000 tons to be named *Oceanic*, but although the keel of this ship, which would have rivalled Cunard's *Queen Mary*, was laid she was never built. Two years later the White Star Line showed a loss for the first time in its history, and following the imprisonment of Lord Kylsant for issuing a false prospectus, the Royal Mail Steam Packet Co. collapsed. The Cunard Steam-Ship Co. were also in difficulties, with work stopped on the building of the *Queen Mary* because of the depression, and it was at this point that the Government stepped in with an offer to save both of Britain's premier shipping lines. Basically it was that the Government would advance

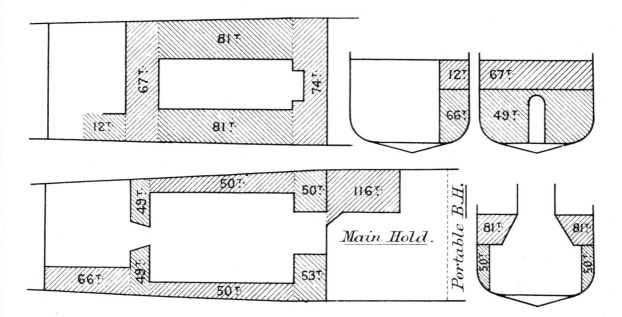

Builder's plan of the *Atlantic's* coal bunkers. Credit: White Star Line.

money for the completion of the *Queen Mary* if Cunard and White Star would amalgamate. And so, in 1934, there came into being the Cunard White Star Line, with Cunard holding 62 per cent of the shares and the Oceanic Steam Navigation Co. 38 per cent. It was virtually the end of the White Star Line and the company which had been registered as White Star Line Ltd. by Lord Kylsant was compulsorily wound up by a High Court order in 1936, the investigation showing a total deficiency of £11 mn. The old White Star ships retained their names under the new management, and even flew the White Star houseflag above Cunard's, but no new ships were added with the White Star style of nomenclature. The Oceanic Steam Navigation Co. was dissolved in August, 1939, the O.S.N. Realisation Co. being formed to look after the interests of the creditors. The Second World War interrupted the proceedings but in 1947 the Cunard Steam-Ship Co. bought out the balance of the shares they did not already own in Cunard White Star, so that the company became a wholly owned subsidiary. In 1949, Cunard announced that they were reverting to their former title, and White Star disappeared completely from the North Atlantic.

The Ismays never forgot the *Atlantic*, although they took pains to see that her name was expunged from any company literature in which ships of the fleet might be mentioned. They set aside an amount to pay for the upkeep of the graves and they contributed half to the cost of a monument in memory of those who were lost. When it was unveiled at Terence Bay on December 7, 1915, the words on it read:

Near this spot was wrecked the s.s. Atlantic,
April 1st, 1873, when 562 persons perished,
of whom 277 were interred in this churchyard.
This monument is erected as a sacred
memorial by a few sympathetic friends.
Jesus said:
I am the resurrection and the life.

Appendix "A"

Extract from Memorandum of Survey of the Steamship *Atlantic*

PARTICULARS

Wood or iron?—Iron
Paddle or screw?—Screw
Official Number?—65,851
Port of Registry?—Liverpool
Built?—At Belfast in the year 1871 by Harland & Wolff

	Feet	Tenths
Length	420	0
Breadth	40	9
Depth to main deck	23	4
Depth to spar deck	31	0
Length of engine-room	91	0

	Tons	Hundredths
Gross tonnage	3,707	10
Allowance for engine-room	1,186	27
Allowance for crew space	154	68
Registered tonnage	2,366	15

Registered horsepower—600
Registered owners—Oceanic Steam Navigation Company Ltd., 10, Water Street, Liverpool

ENGINES

Number?—Two
Where built?—Liverpool
When?—1871
By whom?—G. Forrester & Co.
Description?—Compound inverted
Diameter of cylinder?—78 in and 41 in
Length of stroke?—5·0
Revolutions per minute?—50
Indicated horsepower?—3,000
Surface condensers (if any)?—Yes
Multiple of gearing (if any)?—No

Bilge injection?—Two 6 in pipes
Paddle wheels and bearings examined on the . . . .
Screw propeller and bearings examined on—24th December, 1872
All pipes and cocks connected to the hull examined on—24th December, 1872.
Are all the cocks and pipes which pass through the vessel accessible to the engineer—Yes
Number of tubes in condenser—3,840, diameter $\frac{5}{8}$ inside
Length?—8 ft 3 in
Diameter of screw?—22 ft
Pitch?—26 in fine, 31 ft coarse
Diameter of condenser inside?—7 ft 3 in
Size of crankshaft?—18$\frac{3}{4}$ in
Size of screw shaft?—18 in

MAIN BOILERS

Where made?—Liverpool
When?—1871
By whom?—G. Forrester & Co.
Number?—Ten
Description?—Tubular circular top and bottom
Pitch of stays?—9 × 8$\frac{1}{2}$ × 1$\frac{1}{2}$ backs ends, 15 × 12$\frac{1}{2}$ tube plate
Pitch of stays (average)?—10 in, 14 in and 16 in
Sectional diameter?—2$\frac{1}{4}$, 2$\frac{1}{2}$, 1$\frac{1}{4}$
When last repaired?—Never
Date of last internal examination—12th February, 1873
Superheating apparatus (if any)?—Yes

VALVES

Stop valves, No. (if any)?—Fifteen in all
How placed?—On top
Safety valves, No.?—Two on each boiler, and one for superheater
Diameter of each?—Three five-eighths
Weight per square inch?—Seventy
Government safety valves, No.?—Ten
Diameter?—Three five-eighths
Weight per square inch?—Seventy
If fitted to prevent the pressure from being increased when steam is up, and how?—With lock through spindle and cuttle

DONKEY BOILER

If connected with main boiler?—Yes
Age?—1871
Condition?—Good
Diameter?—14 ft × 8 ft 7 in × 8 ft 10 in
No. of safety valves?—Two

Appendix "A"

Diameter of safety valves?—$3\frac{1}{4}$
Pressure?—Seventy

DONKEY OR AUXILIARY BOILER

		Weights	
Diameter of valve	$3\frac{1}{8}$	$25\frac{1}{2}$	$25\frac{1}{2}$
No.	2	$23\frac{1}{4}$	$23\frac{1}{4}$
Area	7·66	$22\frac{1}{2}$	$22\frac{1}{2}$
Fulcrum	$5\frac{1}{8}$	$19\frac{3}{4}$	$19\frac{3}{4}$
Lever	$24\frac{1}{2}$	$5\frac{1}{2}$	$5\frac{1}{2}$
		$96\frac{1}{2}$	$96\frac{1}{2}$

Weight S.V. and lever, $55\frac{3}{4}$
Pressure 66·74 lb per square inch
Height of boiler?—14 ft
Breadth of boiler?—8 ft 7 in
Length of boiler?—8 ft 10 in
      64 tubes, $3\frac{1}{2}$ in diameter
      30 tubes, $3\frac{3}{4}$ in diameter
Stays?—30 in number
Furnaces?—6 ft 6 in length
Diameter?—3 ft 2 in
      In steam chest:
Four gusset stays, $\frac{5}{8}$ in thick
Four cross stays, $3\frac{1}{2}$ in diameter
Five rows of cross stays on the flat part of each boiler, with extra thickness plates inside and outside, long laps double-rivetted (not chain), and two safety valves on each boiler
Engine-room pumps from each compartment, two Gwynne's pumps, having each 6 in suction pipes, discharge about 50 tons per minute combined
Main engines, bilge pumps can pump from each compartment, suction pipes large enough to supply water to both main engine pumps and donkey engine

GAUGES

No. and description of steam gauges?—Thirteen
No. and description of vacuum gauges?—Four

SURVEY

General condition of hull?—Good
When was bottom last inspected?—December, 1872
What repairs were last executed?—Nil
In what condition are the floor planks?—Good
Are all the keelsons and stringers in good order?—Yes
Are the beams in good order?—Yes

Appendix "A"

Does the vessel show any symptoms of weakness?—No

Are the decks in good order?—Yes

Are the coamings high enough?—Yes

Are the skylights securely fitted?—Yes

Are there shutters to them for bad weather?—Yes

Can the bunker openings be securely closed?—Yes

Are all openings to stoke-holes and places below properly protected from the sea?—Yes

Are the deck houses strongly built?—Yes

Is the front of the poop strongly built?—Nil

Is there a solid or a gutter waterway?—Gutter

Are the side ports and ports fitted with deadlights or plugs?—Yes

Remarks:

Spar deck in three watertight compartments. One at the fore part of the saloon, and one at after part of engine-room; seven watertight bulkheads.

Three decks.

Two iron decks, complete plating in spar deck, $\frac{7}{16}$ thick, main deck plating $\frac{6}{16}$ thick.

Corner of hatches and engine-room doubling plates riveted on top of iron deck to make up strength of section of iron.

(signed)   W. H. Bisset

Surveyor for the Liverpool district

Appendix "B"

Summary of Coal Consumption from Chief Engineer's Logs

Voyage	Old stock	Received in Liverpool	Received abroad	Consumed	Remaining
1*					
2	150	1,018	170	1,328	10
3	30	1,199	200	1,307	97†
4	90	1,177	147	1,338	70
5	60	1,106	350	1,459	57
6*					
7 Out*					
7 Home	77	1,293	232	1,562	40
8 Out*					
8 Home	190		610	709	91
9 Out	90	818		868	40
9 Home*					
10 Out	90	814		719	185
10 Home	185		610	666	129
11 Out	125	1,278		611	792
11 Home	792			575	217
12 Out	320	1,004		634	690
12 Home	690			498	192
13 Out	192	860		654	398
13 Home	398		300	658	40
14 Out	40	956		738	258
14 Home	258		497	645	110
15 Out	110	752		659	203
15 Home	203		560	662	101
16 Out	101	916		777	240
16 Home	240		572	666	146
17 Out	146	1,106		870	382
17 Home*					
18 Out	20	1,133		$816\frac{3}{4}$	$336\frac{1}{4}$
18 Home*					
19 Out					

* Abstract missing   † Mathematically incorrect

It can be seen that different chief engineers adopted different methods of keeping their logs. Under George Watson and George Herriot on Voyages 1 to 5, total figures are given for the round voyage, out and home. The "old stock" here refers to the amount remaining at the end of the homeward voyage, that is, the coal still left in the bunkers when the *Atlantic* arived back in Liverpool. The same system may have been adopted for Voyage 6, the log for which was not found, but on Voyage 7, with Andrew Duncan in charge of the engine-room, the outward and homeward voyages were entered separately but the totals were carried to the homeward abstract. Thereafter, the outward and homeward voyages were kept completely separate and "old stock" at the start of the homeward voyage is the amount remaining on arrival in New York.

For example, at the start of Voyage 16 the *Atlantic* had 101 tons left from Voyage 15 and loaded a further 916 tons in Liverpool. Out of the total of 1,017 tons she consumed 777 tons and therefore had 240 tons left when she arrived at New York. This 240 tons appears as "old stock" on Voyage 16 (home). She loaded 572 tons in New York, burned 666 tons on the way back, and arrived with 146 tons (240 + 572 − 666).

The abstract of the engineer's log for voyage 18 (out) is given on the following pages.

Appendix "B"
WHITE STAR LINE

OCEANIC STEAM NAVIGATION COMPANY, *Ismay, Imrie & Co.*, 10, Water Street, Liverpool.

Abstract of the Engineers' Log of the Steam Ship *Atlantic*—Eighteenth Voyage

Date	Draft of water Forward	Draft of water Aft	Wind ahead, abeam, or free, etc. Rough Sea, etc.	Hours steaming	Hours steam up	Pressure of steam in lb on Safety Valve	Vacuum in Condenser in inches of Mercury	Revolution per minute	Revolutions in 24 hours, or during the time mentioned
	Ft in	Ft in		H. M.	H. M.	lb	in		
Liverpool to New York, *via* Queenstown 1873	21 6	24 5							
14 Feb			Abeam	21 30	24 0	53	25	38·6	49,600
15 Feb			Various	24 30	24 30	54	25	38	56,550
16 Feb			Various, rough sea	24 30	24 30	53	24	39·25	58,450
17 Feb			Various, rough sea	24 20	24 20	53	24½	37·77	55,150
18 Feb			Various, rough sea	24 16	24 16	50	25	34·2	47,870
19 Feb			Various, rough sea	24 30	24 30	51	25	35·8	52,600
20 Feb			Various, rough sea	24 30	24 30	50·6	25	37·59	53,660
21 Feb			Ahead, rough sea	24 15	24 15	52	25	35·5	50,290
22 Feb			Ahead, rough sea	24 30	24 30	52·25	24½	36·6	53,200
23 Feb			Ahead, rough sea	24 30	24 30	51	25	34·58	50,440
24 Feb			Ahead, rough sea	24 30	24 30	51	25	35·2	50,900
25 Feb			Ahead, rough sea	24 30	24 30	50	25	32·9	47,410
26 Feb			Ahead, st. breeze	24 25	24 25	50·8	25	35·38	50,970
Arrival at New York 27 Feb			Various, light	8 50	24 0	53	25	37·9	20,090
				Total 323 30	Total 341 15	Average 51·76	Average 25	Average 35·9	Total 697,180

Miles 3,098

Average per hour 9·5

11·72 per counter

	Coals		Oil	Tallow
	tons	cwt	galls	lb
Old Stock	20	0	113	112
Received in Liverpool	1,133	0	600	62
Total Consumption	816	15	315½	50
Remaining on Board	336	5	397½	

John Foxley, Chief Engineer

continued opposite

Liverpool to New York, *via* Queenstown

Date (1873)	Consumption of stores					Distance in 24 hours by log or observation (Miles)	Distances by Engines (Miles)	Slip per cent	Remarks on Engines, Boilers, Coals, etc
	Coals average in 24 hours, or during the time mentioned (tns cwt)	Coals per hour (cwt)	Quality	Tallow in 24 hours, or during the time mentioned (lb)	Oil in 24 hours, or during the time mentioned (gall)				
14 Feb	53 15	50	Bad	10	29	251	277	11	12 noon full speed from Liverpool. Arrived Queenstown, 7.25 a.m.; 10.20 left, full speed. Bilge pumps to Nos. 1, 2, 3, and 5 holds each watch.
15 Feb	61 5	50	Bad	4	27	282	301	11	
16 Feb	61 5	50	Bad	4	24	281	326	10	
17 Feb	61 2	50	Bad	4	24	273	308	10	
18 Feb	61 5	50	Bad	4	22½	212	264	20	
19 Feb	61 5	50	Bad	4	24	291	290	—	3 p.m., fire in port bunker, fore-end.
20 Feb	61 2	50	Bad	4	24	288	280	3·3	
21 Feb	61 5	50	Bad	4	24	182	280	40	
22 Feb	61 5	50	Bad	4	24	201	290	30·6	10.30 a.m., fire in port bunker, after-end. 7 p.m., fire in starboard bunker, after-end.
23 Feb	61 5	50	Bad	4	22	176	280	6·3	7 a.m., fire in port bunker.
24 Feb	61 5	50	Bad	4	20½	155	280	51	
25 Feb	61 5	50	Bad	4	20½	160	248	30·6	
26 Feb	61 5	50	Bad	4	22	216	280	25·5	
Arrived at New York 27 Feb	22 10	50	Bad	4	8	110	112	11·2	Arrived at Sandy Hook, 7.50. Come to anchor, 8.50 p.m. (46 gallons of oil used in port. Engines and boilers working well. Coals all out from back of port boilers; all English coals.)
	Total 810 19	Average 50	Bad	Total 62	Total 315½	Total 3,098	Total 3,816	Average 20·24	

67

Appendix "C"

Papers Relating to the Loss of the *Atlantic*

Statement of Mr. T. H. Ismay read to the Court of Inquiry.

It is not the fact that the mixed coals were used from motives of economy, but principally on the recommendations of Captain Murray and Mr. Heriot, that better results were obtained from using them, than from South Wales coal entirely.

Captain Murray and Mr. Heriot have given evidence to this effect.

It is not the fact that we have only used mixed coals since the 1st of January.

It has been used, more or less, since the commencement of the line, at various times, as appears from the particulars now handed in.

We bought the Lancashire coal, which we used with the Welsh coal supplied under the contract, in the market, from time to time, from various dealers and colliery proprietors at various prices, particulars of which are handed in. (See opposite page.)

I am informed, and believe, that a considerable portion of the South Wales coal supplied to us, prior to the 1st January last, actually came from the same colliery as that which we have used since that date.

I have also been informed, and believe, that Messrs. Richards Power & Co. have been in the habit of supplying coal directly or indirectly to the several steamship companies, the names of which I hand in.

Cunard Company.   Liverpool and Texas Company.

National Company.   H. N. Hughes and Nephew.

Mississippi and Dominion Company.

As regards the old stock with which the 18th voyage was commenced, I find that the estimate of 20 tons was after the bunkers had all been cleaned out, and consumption in port allowed for.

In considering what is a sufficient supply of coal, I respectfully submit that the Court should have regard to the quick passages made by the vessels of the White Star Line. I beg to hand in a comparative statement of the passages for the first three months of 1872, and the first three months of 1873. (See page 70.)

I submit that regard should also be had to the fact, no other vessel of the Line ever had to put in port for coal. I hand in a list of the vessels which have had to do so during the 12 months prior to the loss of the *"Atlantic."* (See page 70.)

Papers Relating to the Loss of the *Atlantic*

Description and Price of Coal Supplied to the Steamship *Atlantic* on her Different Voyages

Voyage	Tons	Supplier	s.	d.
1	Coaled in Belfast; put on board in Liverpool 271 tons		16	3
2	1,018	Battersby	16	3
3	1,209	Battersby	17	0
	20	Old Stock		
4	1,177	Battersby	18	0
5	520	Battersby	18	0
	273	Powell Duffryn		
	206	Wigan Company, Lancashire	10	0
	60	Old Stock	10	0
6	1,007	Risca	18	9
	124	Powell Duffryn	17	9
	95	Lancashire		
	40	Old Stock		
7	1,224	Powell Duffryn	17	9
	69	Forwood, Paton & Co.		
	77	Old Stock		
8	674	Nixon's Navigation	19	0
	115	Pilkington, Lancashire		
	163	Smith, Lancashire		
	40	Old Stock		
9	723	Barnes, South Wales	19	0
	95	Evans, Lancashire	11	0
	90	Old Stock		
10	182	South Wales		
	546	Powell Duffryn	21	0
	83	Evans, Lancashire	11	0
	90	Old Stock		
11	1,278	Battersby, South Wales	21	6
	125	Old Stock		
12	1,004	Battersby, South Wales	23	0
	320	Old Stock		
13	820	Powell Duffryn	23	0
	40	Battersby, South Wales		
	192	Old Stock		
14	956	Powell Duffryn	25	4
	40	Old Stock		
15	752	Powell Duffryn	25	4
	150	Old Stock		
16	851	Powell Duffryn	25	4
	68	Rea		
	101	Old Stock		
17	989	Powell Duffryn	25	4
	117	Aberdare, Richards, Power & Co.	20	0
	146	Old Stock		
18	439	Lancashire ⎱ Richards,	20	0
	696	South Wales ⎰ Power & Co.		
	20	Old Stock		
19	74	Lancashire		
	249	Lancashire & South Wales ⎱	20	0
	524	South Wales ⎰		
	120	Old Stock		

Papers Relating to the Loss of the *Atlantic*

Comparative Average Passages of Atlantic Steamers

Line	Average per voyage inwards			Favour of White Star			Average per voyage outwards			Favour of White Star		
	D.	H.	M.	D.	H.	M.	D.	H.	M.	D.	H.	M.
Cunard	10	08	22	0	13	27	9	02	12	0	5	17
Inman	11	00	45	1	05	50	10	04	16	1	7	21
National	12	09	06	2	14	11	10	19	38	1	22	43
Guion	12	11	47	2	16	52	10	18	08	1	21	13
White Star	9	18	55				8	20	55			
Cunard (No. 2)	12	03	06	2	08	11	10	04	16	1	7	21
Bremen	11	19	06	2	00	11	10	10	14	1	15	19
Hamburg	11	21	30	2	02	35	9	20	24	0	23	29
Anchor	13	10	34	3	15	39	12	15	25	3	11	20

Notes: Cunard, Inman, National and White Star Lines are calculated between Roche's Point and Sandy Hook. The Saturday boats from Liverpool, and Wednesday boats hence of the Cunard Line, and the Thursday boats from Liverpool, and Saturday boats hence of the Inman Line, only are included from January to August.
Cunard Line (No. 2) calculated between Boston and Roche's Point.
Bremen Line calculated between Sandy Hook and Southampton.
Hamburg Line calculated between Sandy Hook and Plymouth.
(The averages of the two latter include only voyages since August.)
Anchor Line calculated between Sandy Hook and Moville, from 1st August to 31st December.

List of Vessels Which Have Had to Put Into Port Short of Coal

Steamer	Date	Line
Britannia	January, 1872	Anchor
Cuba	March, 1872	Cunard
Silesia	November, 1872	Hamburg
Queen	December, 1872	National
Siberia	December, 1872	Cunard
Cuba	December, 1872	Cunard
Glamorgan	December, 1872	Cardiff
Idaho	January, 1873	Guion
Minnesota	January, 1873	Guion
Cuba	February, 1873	Cunard
America	February, 1873	Bremen
*City of Washington**	January, 1873	Inman

* *City of Washington* put into Boston.

Appendix "D"

An Appreciation of the *Atlantic's* Engines

by G. J. A. White, B. Sc., C.Eng., A.M.I.Mech.E., A.M.I.Mar.E., M.R.I.N.

FOR any reciprocating steam engine it is possible to construct a Hypothetical Indicator Diagram if one knows the steam and condenser pressures and the point at which the steam is cut off. Such a diagram implies the following:

(a) Steam is admitted to the cylinder at boiler pressure, the piston moving down the cylinder until

(b) the cut-off point is reached. The piston continues to move, the steam now expanding according to the law PV = constant. This is known as hyperbolic expansion, since the curve of PV = constant is a hyperbola.

(c) When the piston is at full stroke, the pressure falls instantaneously to condenser pressure and remains there whilst

(d) the piston returns to its original position.

Figure 1 shows such a diagram.

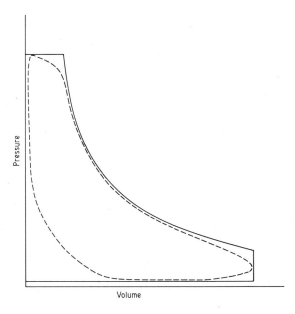

Figure 1

71

Appendix "D"

The area of such a diagram represents the maximum amount of work which could possibly be done by a particular engine working between the given limits of pressure (boiler and condenser) and at the given cut-off. In practice, the area of the diagram, and hence the work done, falls short of this for a number of reasons.

(1) Steam will only flow from boiler to cylinder, and from cylinder to condenser, if a difference of pressure exists. Hence the pressure during the first part of the cycle will be somewhat less than boiler pressure; during the last part it will be a little greater than condenser pressure.

(2) The expansion of steam in a cylinder is a complicated process and a law such as PV = constant can only approximate to the actual process.

(3) The Hypothetical Diagram disregards clearance volume completely. An engine cannot be designed such that, with the piston at an extreme of stroke, the cylinder volume is zero. There must be a working clearance between piston and cylinder cover; in addition, there must be passages between the cylinder and the valve. The latter, plus the working clearance, are referred to as the Clearance Volume and, in a well-designed engine, may amount to some 6 per cent. of the swept volume. At some point during the return stroke, the valve closes to exhaust and the steam remaining in the cylinder is compressed. Ideally, at the end of the stroke, its temperature and pressure should be identical to those of the steam about to enter the cylinder for the next stroke.

(4) The presence, on a Hypothetical Diagram, of a sharp corner implies a valve which opens and closes instantaneously. As no real valve does this, the corners of an actual diagram are rounded.

The effect of this is that an actual diagram is much smaller in area than the Hypothetical one; a typical one is shown dotted in Figure 1 also. The area of the Hypothetical Diagram can be calculated, knowing the dimensions of the engine, the two pressures and the cut-off point; the formula is Area = $P_1 V_1 (1 + \log_e r) - P_2 V_2$, when

$$r = \text{cut-off ratio} = V_2 / V_1 \tag{1}$$

The area of the actual diagram, taken from the engine whilst running, can be measured. The two areas, and hence the amount of work done, are simply related by the notion of a Diagram Factor, thus

Area of actual diagram = Diagram factor × area of Hypothetical Diagram

Exactly the same reasoning may be applied to a compound engine. Figure 2 shows both diagrams. It must be remembered that, in a compound engine, the cut-off in the high pressure cylinder is the factor controlling the area of the diagram.

Typical values for diagram factor are:

Simple expansion	0·76
Compound (2-stage)	0·70
Triple expansion	0·625

A useful concept when dealing with any reciprocating engine, steam or internal combustion, is that of Mean Effective Pressure. The definition of this quantity is that pressure which, acting continuously on a piston during its stroke, would produce the same amount of work as the varying pressure during an actual cycle produces. This is perhaps more clearly seen graphically.

Figure 3 shows a Hypothetical Diagram, the area enclosed by this being the work done. If a rectangle is drawn having the same width and area as the Hypothetical Diagram, then the height of the rectangle is equal to the Mean Effective Pressure.

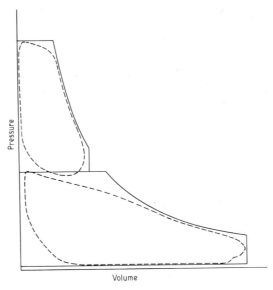

Figure 2

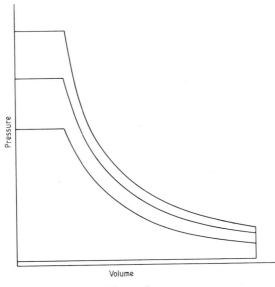

Figure 3

There are various kinds of M.E.P. The one just considered, which applies to a Hypothetical Diagram, is the Hypothetical M.E.P. If an actual diagram were used, then it would be the indicated M.E.P.

One of the uses of M.E.P. is in calculating horsepower. For a working cycle, the work done is equal to the area of the diagram and this is, by definition, equal to the M.E.P. times the swept volume, i.e.,

Work done $W = (M.E.P.) \times$ swept volume

73

Appendix "D"

Now the swept volume is equal to the stroke L times the piston area A, or

$$\text{swept volume} = L \times A$$

hence $W = (\text{M.E.P.}) \times L \times A$

If there are N working strokes per minute, then

$$W/\text{min} = (\text{M.E.P.}) \times L \times A \times N$$

W, of course, will be in ft lb and, since 33,000 ft lb/min equal one horsepower, we may say that

$$\text{Horsepower} = [(\text{M.E.P.}) \times L \times A \times N]/33{,}000$$

If we understand that the symbol P represents Mean Effective Pressure, we have the shorter, more familar form

$$\text{HP} = PLAN/33{,}000 \qquad\qquad (2)$$

For a compound engine, it is possible to calculate a Mean Effective Pressure for each cylinder. Normally, however, we calculate one M.E.P. for the whole engine, on the basis of the volume of the low pressure cylinder; in other words, we "refer" the pressure to the l.p. cylinder volume, thus obtaining a "referred M.E.P.".

We may calculate this quantity by dividing equation (1) by V_2, giving

$$\text{Hypothetical M.E.P.} = (P_1/r)(1 + \log_e r) - P_2 \qquad\qquad (3)$$

We may note that actual M.E.P. = diagram factor × hypothetical M.E.P.

In internal combustion engine practice, the main purpose of M.E.P. is to enable engines of different sizes to be compared. By taking a diagram, the Indicated Mean Effective Pressure is obtained, and this leads to the calculation of Indicated Horsepower, i.e., the horsepower actually developed in the cylinders. The useful output of the engine, of course, is less than this, and is known as Brake Horsepower. By measuring this (by a brake, dynamometer, torsionmeter, etc.) and using the same formula, we may obtain a Brake Mean Effective Pressure. This may appear to be a rather artificial figure, but it represents the pressure which, acting in the cylinder, would give the same brake work as the engine actually produces. Comparison of this figure for different engines gives some indication of the relative mechanical efficiencies of the engines, i.e., the proportion of the power developed in the cylinders which is available to do work.

We may now examine the figures for the *Atlantic* in the light of these formulae. The dimensions are:

Cylinders: 41 in and 78 in × 60 in stroke
Boiler pressure: 70 lb/sq in or 84·7 lb/sq in absolute
Condenser pressure: about 2 lb/sq in absolute
Speed: 50 rev/min or 100 working strokes/min
Cylinder volumes: 45·9 and 165·7 cub ft

Let us start with the quoted figure of 3,000 i.h.p. We do not know whether this is hypothetical or measured but, whichever it is, we apply equation (2) to get

$$3{,}000 = (P \times 165{\cdot}7 \times 100)/33{,}000$$

whence P (the M.E.P.) = 41·5 lb/sq in. If this is, in fact, the hypothetical M.E.P., we use equation (3) to find r. We have

$$(84{\cdot}7/r)(1 + \log_e r) - 2 = 41{\cdot}5$$

whence, by trial and error, r is found to be almost exactly five. Hence V_1, in Figure 1, is equal to one-fifth of V_2 or 33·1 cub ft. As the h.p. volume is 45·9 cub ft, the h.p. cut-off point is

$$(33·1/45·9) = 72 \text{ per cent.}$$

This is shown in Figure 4.

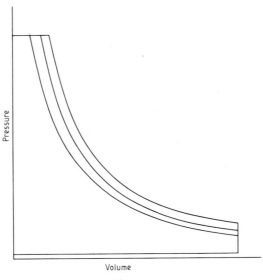

Figure 4

At this point, we may draw some comparisons with information presented in two papers on marine engineering, given in 1872 and 1881. I have extracted details of four ships from Bramwell's paper, having cylinder dimensions somewhere near those of the *Atlantic*; he quotes no ship having a stroke greater than 50 in. From Marshall, I have taken two; one with almost identical bores, the other with the same stroke but greater bores.

The *Atlantic's* dimensions, as might be expected from her building date, are closer to Marshall's figures than to Bramwell's, though, for her bore size, she had a comparatively long stroke. What is quite apparent is that the figure of 41·5 lb/sq in for M.E.P. is out of this world. Even assuming that it is hypothetical M.E.P., the indicated M.E.P. would be 29 lb/sq in. The M.E.P. is never more than a third of the working pressure, and the one example with an i.h.p. comparable with the *Atlantic's* quoted figure has very much larger cylinders. All one can say is that her engine *could* have developed 3,000 i.h.p. if fed with steam at 70 lb/sq in, but it is highly improbable that her boilers could have produced sufficient steam. Her actual pressure of 54 lb/sq in is in line with the earlier group of ships (1872), whereas the figure of 70 lb/sq in is nearer to the 1881 group. However, the expansion ratio of five, calculated from the 70 lb/sq in, is about right for her actual pressure, according to Marshall, who quotes a value of 7·05 as typical for a boiler pressure of 77 lb/sq in.

Her condenser area is also interesting. Marshall states that practice then was to provide 2 sq ft/i.h.p., though he himself had found that 1·4 sq ft/i.h.p. was sufficient to maintain $27\frac{1}{2}$ in of vacuum. If we assume that the actual steam expansion follows the law $PV = $ constant, we can calculate, for $r = 5$, the pressure in the l.p. cylinder when the valve opens to exhaust. This is 16·9 lb/sq in absolute, i.e., it is above atmospheric, which would lead to most inefficient working.

The next step is to take the actual working pressure of 54 lb/sq in (68·7 lb/sq in absolute) and evaluate the i.h.p., assuming $r = 5$. We find that Hypothetical M.E.P. = 33·9 lb/sq in and Hypothetical i.h.p. = 2,450. Assuming a diagram factor of 0·7, the actual M.E.P. and i.h.p. figures are 23·7 lb/sq in and 1,715, which are much more realistic. However, the coal consumption now becomes gross, 3·27 lb/i.h.p. hr at 60 tons/day and 3·8 lb/i.h.p. hr at 70 tons/day. This could be explained by reference to her condenser, however. The area, for 1,715 i.h.p., is a little over 3 sq ft/i.h.p. This would undoubtedly mean that the condensed steam would be cooled to well below its condensation temperature. Ideally, the condenser should condense the steam without cooling the condensate, so that the latter may be returned to the boiler at the highest possible temperature. If it does undercool the condensate, then the boiler has to provide additional heat in order to heat the feed water.

If we now look at a hypothetical diagram based on 54 lb/sq in (Figure 5), we find that, at 72 per cent. cut-off, the cylinder pressure at exhaust is now 13·75 lb/sq in. This is still high, but much more realistic. We could expect the actual (as opposed to the hypothetical) figure to be some 8–9 lb/sq in. If the point of cut-off is advanced, as suggested in the evidence, to three-quarters of its original value, then we have a value of r of 6·7, which gives a pressure of

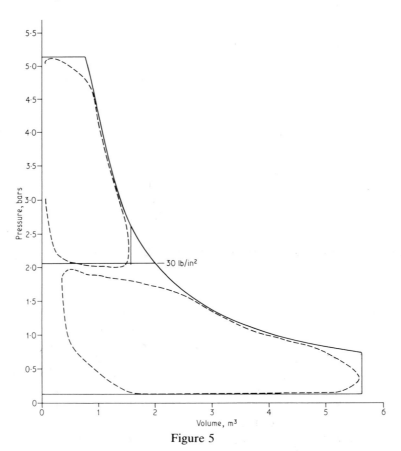

Figure 5

10·25 lb/sq. in. At the minimum realistic pressure of, say, 5 lb/sq in, r becomes 13·75, with the cut-off at 26·5 per cent., though one would not try and work at such a low cut-off figure.

Tabulating the M.E.Ps corresponding to these cut-off figures, we have:

Cut-off %	M.E.P. lb/in	Relative to 72% c-o: Cut-off %	M.E.P. lb/in
72	33·9	1	1
54	27·8	0·75	0·82
26·5	16·1	0·368	0·475

One must be careful in drawing conclusions from these figures. It is apparent, that, as the cut-off is reduced, the M.E.P. is reduced, but at a lower rate. *If the engine speed remains constant,* then, as steam consumption is proportional to cut-off, it is much more efficient to work at a reduced cut-off value. However, as the cut-off value is reduced, the speed will certainly fall and one cannot infer more without some knowledge of the actual speeds.

One may sum up as follows:

(1) The quoted figure of 3,000 i.h.p. is quite unrealistic. The engine *could* deliver this, if supplied with sufficient steam at 70 lb/sq in, but the evidence at the inquiry suggests that the boilers could not do this.

(2) To make further calculations, the expansion ratio r must be known. To arrive at a figure of 3,000 i.h.p. r must have been taken as 5. This value is realistic for a ship of her age (though not for her quoted boiler pressure) and is therefore used here.

(3) Taking r as 5 and working pressure as 54 lb/sq in, the actual i.h.p. is about 1,715. This implies an M.E.P. of 23·7 lb/sq in, more in line with practice at that time.

(4) The coal consumption, 3·27 lb/i.h.p. hr, is excessive, average figures given in the papers for 1872 and 1881 being 2·11 and 1·878 lb/i.h.p. hr.

(5) The condenser area is appropriate to the quoted i.h.p., suggesting that the engine was intended for use with larger, or more numerous, boilers, delivering steam at 70 lb/sq in.

(6) The excessive condenser area would result in excessive coal consumption. The comparatively great stroke/bore ratio, leading to inefficient use of steam, together with the release of steam from the l.p. cylinder at too high a pressure, would also produce high fuel consumption.

Papers Relating to the Loss of the *Atlantic*

Reference	Cylinders		Stroke in	Speed rev/min	Steam Pressure			Coal Con-sumption ton/i.h.p. hr	Con-denser Area sq ft.
	Diameter h.p. in	l.p. in			Boiler lb/in^2	M.E.P. lb/in^2	i.h.p.		
Bramwell 1	42	75	42	47	58	18·1	793	2·80	
Bramwell 2	45	80	36	51	51	17·6	825	2·60	
Bramwell 12	46	82	48	54	54	20·0	1,394	2·01	
Bramwell 18	44	78	42	55	60	17·2	964	1·70	
Atlantic	41	78	60	50	70	41·5[1] / 23·7[2]	3,000[1] / 1,715[2]	1·87[3,1] / 3·27[3,2]	5,190
Marshall 2	42	80	48	69	72·5	22·3	1,881	1·60	
Marshall 15	51	88	60	59	75	23·6	2,745	1·83	5,000

Notes: [1] Quoted: hypothetical   [2] Calculated   [3] At 60 tons/day

References: Bramwell, F. J.: On the Progress Effected in Economy of Fuel in Steam Navigation, Considered in Relation to Compound-Cylinder Engines and High-Pressure Steam. Proc. I. Mech.E., 1872.
Marshall, F. C.: On the Progress and Development of the Marine Engine. Proc. I. Mech.E., 1881.